EVERYTHING®
Series

Dear Reader,

Ciao! And a heartfelt *grazie* for picking up *The Everything® Italian Phrase Book*, my second book with Adams Media.

My passion for the Italian language and culture started when I was very young. My maternal grandfather, Eugenio Savastano, was born in Italy, in a small town in the Provincia di Caserta called Orchi. Though he died when I was very young, my memories of him as a kind and gentle man are indelible. Never wanting to forget my grandfather, I suppose my passion for everything Italian is my way of keeping his memory alive, and honoring the family legacy that he left behind.

I've been studying, teaching, and speaking Italian for about twenty-five years. Hopefully, some of my passion (and experiences!) will come through in this book. Try hard to use as much Italian as you can when traveling—you'll find that Italians are generally very receptive to your efforts to speak their language.

Ronald Glenn Wrigley

The EVERYTHING Series

These handy, accessible books give you all you need to tackle a difficult project, gain a new hobby, or even brush up on something you learned back in school but have since forgotten. You can read from cover to cover or just pick out information from our four useful boxes.

 Alerts: Urgent warnings

 Essentials: Quick handy tips

 Facts: Important snippets of information

 Questions: Answers to common questions

When you're done reading, you can finally say you know **EVERYTHING**®!

PUBLISHER Karen Cooper

DIRECTOR OF ACQUISITIONS AND INNOVATION Paula Munier

MANAGING EDITOR, EVERYTHING SERIES Lisa Laing

COPY CHIEF Casey Ebert

ACQUISITIONS EDITOR Lisa Laing

SENIOR DEVELOPMENT EDITOR Elizabeth Kassab

EDITORIAL ASSISTANT Hillary Thompson

Visit the entire Everything® series at *www.everything.com*

THE
EVERYTHING®
ITALIAN
PHRASE
BOOK

A quick refresher for any situation

Ronald Glenn Wrigley, M.A.

Aadamsmedia
Avon, Massachusetts

An Everything® Series Book.
Everything® and everything.com® are registered trademarks of
F+W Media, Inc.

Published by Adams Media, an F+W MEdia Company
57 Littlefield Street, Avon, MA 02322 U.S.A.
www.adamsmedia.com

ISBN 10: 1-59869-756-0
ISBN 13: 978-1-59869-756-8

Printed in Canada.

J I H G F E D C B A

Library of Congress Cataloging-in-Publication Data
available from the publisher.

This publication is designed to provide accurate and authoritative information
with regard to the subject matter covered. It is sold with the understanding
that the publisher is not engaged in rendering legal, accounting, or other
professional advice. If legal advice or other expert assistance is required, the
services of a competent professional person should be sought.
  —From a *Declaration of Principles* jointly adopted by a Committee
of the American Bar Association and a Committee of Publishers and
Associations

Many of the designations used by manufacturers and sellers to distinguish
their products are claimed as trademarks. Where those designations appear
in this book and Adams Media was aware of a trademark claim, the designations have been printed with initial capital letters.

This book is available at quantity discounts for bulk purchases.
For information, please call 1-800-289-0963.

Visit the entire Everything® series at www.everything.com

Dedication

For Ellen and Matthew

Acknowledgments

Many thanks to my beautiful wife, Ellen,
for her support, to Matthew for his good cheer,
and to my family for their inspiration.
And many thanks to Lisa Laing and Elizabeth Kassab,
and to all of the folks at Adams, for their
guidance along the way.

Contents

Introduction

Forty million tourists visit Italy each year. Two of Italy's major cities—Florence and Rome—are among the most visited cities in the world. On any given day of the year, this equates to 110,000 foreign tourists in Italy. Many travel guides recommend that tourists make an effort to get off the beaten path; to find that small, out-of-the-way place that few tourists ever visit. It is in these areas where the "real" Italy can be experienced; it is also in these areas where very little English is spoken by the general population. This book will be very useful for the 110,000 foreign tourists who hope to have a unique, off-the-beaten-path experience in Italy.

This book will be a useful tool to help integrate both the inexperienced and experienced traveler into many essential aspects of daily life. For these tourists, a very basic understanding of the language can enhance their stay in Italy. Italians treasure politeness, and everywhere in the world people can appreciate the good manners of a "thank you" or "you're welcome." Italians will respond to your efforts to communicate in their language with wholehearted appreciation. By making an effort to learn some basic phrases and expressions, you will feel safer and more assured to take the path less traveled, you will discover useful and interesting facts, you will cope with unexpected situations, and you will be greeted with much greater kindness.

This book will also be a useful resource for high school and college students who wish to enhance their in-class learning experiences. It will be a handy resource to help students sharpen their speaking ability by learning useful expressions (and their correct pronunciation) that pertain to everyday life.

The Everything® Italian Phrase Book offers grammar and pronunciation sections for easier, more effective use and contains essential information for first-time and experienced travelers alike. It features more than 1,400 words and phrases, covering all subjects that people are likely to encounter in their travels—from reserving a hotel room or ordering dinner at a restaurant to using a cell phone or changing a flight. There is also a detailed phonetic pronunciation table plus an extensive word list and grammar guide that will enable travelers to construct basic sentences.

Chapter 1

Introduction to Italian

Italian is a Romance language spoken by about 63 million people in Italy and parts of Switzerland. Modern standard Italian was adopted by the Italian government after the unification of Italy in about 1871 and has its roots in the region of Tuscany, in central Italy. There are many dialects of Italian spoken throughout the Italian peninsula. Dialects are generally not used for purposes of mass communication and are usually spoken in local, informal contexts by native speakers. Most all Italians speak a dialect (Venetian, Neapolitan, Sicilian, etc.), but they can easily switch to standard Italian.

Reading and Pronouncing Italian

Italian is based on a twenty-one-letter alphabet. Though you will come across the letters J, K, W, X, and Y in your travels, you will notice that these letters only appear in words borrowed from other languages (*whiskey* and *jolly*, to name a few). English and Italian share many cognates—words that are spelled similarly in the two languages. Some of these words are modern and are related to recent technology: *telefono, calcolatrice, macchina.* You will recognize many words related to musical terminology (*alto, soprano, trombone*) and to cuisine as well (*al dente, biscotti, pepperoni*).

-FACT

> The vowels *a* and *e* can have two slightly different pronunciations. There is no way to tell by looking at a written word which pronunciation to use. *Pesca* (peach) is spelled the exact same way as *pesca* (fishing). There is a very slight pronunciation difference between the two: *pesca* (pronounced PAYS-ca) means fishing, *pesca* (pronounced PESS-ca) means peach.

Pronunciation Guide

Italian Letter(s)	English representation	Comparable English Pronunciation	Example in Italian
A	ahh	as in far	*alta*
B	b	as in boy	*bello*

Italian Letter(s)	English representation	Comparable English Pronunciation	Example in Italian
C	chi	as *ch* in children when followed by *e* or *i*	*Cina*, Gucci
	k	as *k* in keep when followed by *he* or *hi*	*chi, bruschetta*
	k	as *kee* in keep when followed by *a, o,* or *u*	*caro, scopo, scuba*
	k	as *kee* in keep when followed by a consonant	*criminale*
	sh	as *sh* in she when preceded by s and followed by *i* or *e*	*scelta, sci*
D	d	as in David	*dormo*
E	e	as in elf	*elefante*
F	f	as in father	*fare*
G	j	as *j* in gem or jeep when followed by *e* or *i*	*gelato, giorno*
	g	as *g* in go when followed by *he* or *hi*	*spaghetti, paghi*
	g	as *g* in go when followed by *a, o,* or *u*	*gastronomia, lago,* Gucci
	lli	as *lli* in million when followed by *l*	*figlio, aglio, famiglia*
	ni	as *ni* in onion when followed by *n*	*gnocchi, ognuno, signore*
H	always silent *spaghetti, hotel*		*hanno*
I	ee	as in meet	*Italia*
L	l	as *l* in love	*Lucca*
M	m	as *m* in meet	*Marco*
N	n	as *n* in nice	*Napoli*

Italian Letter(s)	English representation	Comparable English Pronunciation	Example in Italian
O	o	as *o* in loan	*Como*
P	p	as *p* in Peter	*pizza*
Q	qu	as *qu* in quick	*questo*
R	r	as *r* in ladder	*raro*
S	s/z	as in hose when it is between two vowels	*casa*
	s/z	as in hose when it begins a word and is immediately followed by *b, d, g, l, m, n, r,* or *v*	*sbadiglio, smettere*
	s	as in sky elsewhere	*sasso, sentire*
T	t	as *t* in time	*teatro*
U	oo	as *oo* in cool	*uno*
V	v	as *v* in victory	*vittoria*
Z	ts	as *tz* in pretzel	*pizza*
	ds	as *ds* in lads	*zero*

In addition to the twenty-one Italian letters, there are five foreign letters, used in words borrowed from other languages.

Foreign Letters

Italian Letter(s)	Italian Pronunciation	Comparable English Pronunciation	Example in Italian
J	*i lunga*	as *j* in joy	*jolly*
K	*cappa*	as *k* in key	*kiwi*
W	*doppia vu*	as *w* in whiskey	*whiskey*
X	*ics*	as *x* in extra	*mixer*
Y	*ipsilon*	as *y* in yogurt	*yogurt*

-**QUESTION**

How can I practice my pronunciation?
Pronunciation isn't something that can be learned from a book, and learning to speak Italian won't come from reading a book. Hire a native speaker as a tutor, watch Italian movies, and listen to Italian music to develop an ear for spoken Italian.

Double Consonants

Native speakers of English often have great difficulty in mastering the pronunciation of double consonants in Italian. One rule to keep in mind in learning correct pronunciation is that every letter in an Italian word must be pronounced. With this in mind, it logically follows that double consonants are pronounced longer than single consonants:

sano (pronounced sa-no) / *sanno* (pronounced san-no)
lego (pronounced le-go) / *leggo* (pronounced leg-go)
fata (pronounced fa-ta) / *fatta* (pronounced fat-ta)
papa (pronounced pa-pa) / *pappa* (pronounced pap-pa)

The double *s* in Italian has a different pronunciation than the single *s*:

casa (here the *s* is pronounced as in the English hose)
cassa (here the *ss* is pronounced as in the English house)

Accent/Stress

Most words in Italian are pronounced with the stress falling on the next-to-last syllable.

amico	*mangiare*	*cartolina*	*volere*
ah-MEE-koh	mahn-JAH-ray	kahr-toh-LEE-nah	vohl-EH-ray

There is also a group of words that are pronounced with the stress falling in the last syllable. All of these words have a written accent:

università	*perché*	*venerdì*	*virtù*
oo-nee-vehr-see-TAH	pehr-KAY	vehn-ehr-DEE	veer-TOO

Many words are pronounced with the stress on the third-to-last or fourth-to-last syllable. There is no rule governing the placement of the stress in these cases. As you develop an ear for the language you will learn which pronunciation sounds better.

facile	*portabile*	*aspettano*
FAH-chee-leh	pohr-TAH-bee-leh	ah-SPEHT-tah-noh

Introduction to Nouns

Singular Nouns

Italian nouns almost always end in a vowel. Those that don't are usually words borrowed from other languages.

Generally speaking, nouns that end in –o are masculine, and words that end in –a are feminine. Nouns ending in –e can be either masculine or feminine. The gender of these nouns must be learned.

libro (masculine)	LEE-broh
casa (feminine)	KAH-zah
madre (feminine)	MAH-dray
padre (masculine)	PAH-dray

-SSENTIAL

When learning a foreign language, you will learn convenient grammatical rules to help you along. It is important to be open-minded. For every rule, there's bound to be an exception. The rules presented here are very basic—you will notice exceptions to these rules throughout the book.

Plural Nouns

Masculine nouns that end in –o form the plural by changing the –o into an –i. Feminine nouns that end in –a form the plural by changing the –o into an –e. Both masculine and feminine nouns that end in –e form the plural by changing the –e into an –i. Here are some examples:

libro (LEE-broh) changes to *libri* (LEE-bree)
amico (ah-MEE-koh) changes to *amici* (ah-MEE-chee)
gatto (GAHT-toh) changes to *gatti* (GAHT-tee)

sorella (soh-REHL-lah) changes to *sorelle* (soh-REHL-leh)

casa (KAH-zah) changes to *case* (KAH-zeh)

tazza (TAHTS-sah) changes to *tazze* (TAHTS-seh)

dottore (doht-TOH-ray) changes to *dottori* (doht-TOH-ree)

stazione (stahts-see-YOH-nay) changes to *stazioni* (stahts-see-YOH-nee)

cane (KAH-neh) changes to *cani* (KAH-nee)

Definite and Indefinite Articles

Nouns often are accompanied by a definite article (corresponds to "the" in English). There are seven definite articles in Italian: *il*, *lo*, *l'*, *la* (singular); *i*, *gli*, *le* (plural). There are four indefinite articles (corresponding to "a" or "an" in English)—*un*, *uno*, *un'*, and *una* are all used before singular nouns. Which definite or indefinite article you choose depends on the number (singular or plural), the gender (masculine or feminine), and the first letter of the word in question.

-SSENTIAL

Italian articles are sometimes difficult to master, because they have to agree with the noun they modify and don't always correspond to articles in other languages. As a general rule, there is almost always an article in front of a noun in Italian, except when indicating a profession. In Italian, "I am a professor" is *Sono professore*.

Indefinite Articles

The indefinite articles *un* and *uno* are used for masculine nouns, and *un'* and *una* are used for feminine nouns. We must look at the first letter of the word in order to come up with the correct form of the indefinite article.

If the first letter of the noun is . . .	Masculine	Feminine
. . . a consonant	*un ragazzo*	*una casa*
	oon rah-GAHTS-so	oo-nah KAH-zah
. . . a vowel	*un amico*	*un'amica*
	oon ah-MEE-koh	oon-ah-MEE-kah
. . . s + consonant	*uno stadio*	*una studentessa*
	oo-noh STAH-dee-yoh	oo-nah stoo-dehn-TESS-ah
. . . z	*uno zero*	*una zebra*
	oo-noh DSEH-roh	oo-nah DSAY-brah

Definite Articles

There are seven forms of the definite article in Italian—*il, l', lo, i, gli* (masculine), and *la, l', le* (feminine).

If the word is feminine, and the first letter of the word is . . .	Singular	Plural
. . . a consonant	*la ragazza*	*le ragazze*
	lah rah-GAHTS-sah	leh rah-GAHTS-seh
. . . a vowel	*l'amica*	*le amiche*
	lah-MEE-kah	leh ah-MEE-keh

If the word is masculine, and the first letter of the word is . . .	Singular	Plural
. . . a consonant	*il libro*	*i libri*
	eel LEE-broh	ee LEE-bree
. . . a vowel	*l'amico*	*gli amici*
	lah-MEE-koh	lyee ah-MEE-chee
. . . *z*	*lo zero*	*gli zeri*
	loh DSEH-roh	lyee DSEH-ree
. . . an *s* + a consonant	*lo studente*	*gli studenti*
	loh stoo-DEHN-teh	lyee stoo-DEHN-tee

Cognates

Learning Italian can be made easier by developing an ability to recognize cognates—words that look like English words and have a meaning similar to those words. There are some patterns to recognize and follow in order to sharpen your ability to recognize and use cognates.

Nouns that end in *–ia* in Italian usually end in *–y* in English.

Spelling Equivalents

Italian word		English equivalent
psicologia	psee-koh-loh-JEE-yah	psychology
autonomia	ou-toh-noh-MEE-yah	autonomy

Nouns that end in *–ica* in Italian usually end in *–ic(s)* in English.

Spelling Equivalents

Italian word		English equivalent
fisica	FEE-zee-kah	physics
musica	MOO-zee-kah	music

Nouns that end in *–tà* in Italian usually end in *–ty* in English.

Spelling Equivalents

Italian word		English equivalent
università	oo-nee-vehr-see-TAH	university
autorità	ahw-toh-ree-TAH	authority

Nouns that end in *–ista* in Italian usually end in *–ist* in English.

Spelling Equivalents

Italian word		English equivalent
dentista	dehn-TEES-tah	dentist
artista	ahr-TEES-tah	artist

Nouns that end in *–ario* in Italian usually end in *–ary* in English.

Spelling Equivalents

Italian word		English equivalent
diario	dee-AH-ree-oh	diary
dizionario	deet-see-oh-NAH-ree-yoh	dictionary

Nouns that end in *–ore* in Italian usually end in *–or* in English.

Spelling Equivalents

Italian word		English equivalent
professore	proh-fess-SOHR-ray	professor
attore	aht-TOHR-ray	actor

Nouns that end in *–ione* in Italian usually end in *–ion* in English.

Spelling Equivalents

Italian word		English equivalent
stazione	stahts-see-YOH-nay	station
religione	reh-lee-JOH-nay	religion

Nouns that end in *–za* in Italian usually end in *–ce* in English.

Spelling Equivalents

Italian word		English equivalent
importanza	eem-pohr-TAHNZ-ah	importance
indipendenza	een-dee-pehn-DEHNZ-ah	independence

Adjectives ending in *–ale* in Italian usually end in *–al* in English.

Spelling Equivalents

Italian word		English equivalent
speciale	speh-CHAH-lay	special
locale	loh-KAH-lay	local

Adjectives ending in *–oso* usually end in *–ous* in English.

Spelling Equivalents

Italian word		English equivalent
religioso	reh-lee-JOH-soh	religious
amoroso	ah-mohr-OH-soh	amorous

False Friends

The following section will help you to avoid many common mistakes. False friends are words that look alike but have different meanings. There are numerous false friends in Italian and English!

-FACT

> There are thousands of cognates between Italian and English, but some of them can be false friends! Make sure you know the true meaning of a word before working it into your spoken language.

False Friends

addizione ≠ addiction ahd-deets-YOH-nay	*addizione* = sum
annoiato ≠ annoyed ahn-noy-YAH-toh	*annoiato* = bored
apprendere ≠ to apprehend ahp-PREHN-deh-ray	*apprendere* = to learn
argomento ≠ argument ahr-goh-MEHN-toh	*argomento* = subject
assistere ≠ to assist ahs-SEES-teh-ray	*assistere* = to attend
asso ≠ ass ahss-soh	*asso* = ace
attendere ≠ to attend aht-TEHN-deh-ray	*attendere* = to wait
attualmente ≠ actually aht-too-ahl-MEHN-tay	*attualmente* = currently
baldo ≠ bald BAHL-doh	*baldo* = courageous
bravo ≠ brave BRAH-voh	*bravo* = good/clever
camera ≠ camera KAH-meh-rah	*camera* = room
cantina ≠ canteen kahn-TEE-nah	*cantina* = cellar
caldo ≠ cold KAHL-doh	*caldo* = hot
collegio ≠ college kohl-LEH-jee-yoh	*collegio* = boarding school

False Friends

comprensivo ≠ comprehensive kohm-prehn-SEE-voh	*comprensivo* = understanding
concorrenza ≠ concurrence kohn-kohr-REHN-Zah	*concorrenza* = competition
cocomero ≠ cucumber koh-KOH-meh-roh	*cocomero* = watermelon
delusione ≠ delusion deh-looz-YOH-nay	*delusione* = disappointment
disgrazia ≠ disgrace dees-GRAHTS-see-yah	*disgrazia* =misfortune
editore = editor eh-dee-TOH-ray	*editore* = publisher
educato ≠ educated eh-doo-KAH-toh	*educato* = polite
eventualmente ≠ eventually eh-vehn-too-ahl-MEHN-tay	*eventualmente* = possibly, if necessary
fabbrica ≠ fabric FAHB-bree-kah	*fabbrica* = factory
fattoria ≠ factory faht-toh-REE-yah	*fattoria* = farm
inabitato ≠ inhabited een-ah-bee-TAH-toh	*inabitato* = uninhabited
genitore ≠ janitor jeh-nee-TOH-ray	*genitore* = parent
parente ≠ parent pah-REHN-tay	*parente* = relative

False Friends

largo ≠ large LAHR-goh	*largo* = wide
lettura ≠ lecture leht-TOO-rah	*lettura* = reading
libreria ≠ library lee-breh-REE-yah	*libreria* = bookstore
licenziare ≠ to license lee-chenz-YAH-ray	*licenziare* = to dismiss, to fire
lussuria ≠ luxury loos-soo-REE-yah	*lussuria* = lust
magazzino ≠ magazine mah-gahts-SEE-noh	*magazzino* = warehouse
messa ≠ mess MEHSS-sah	*messa* = mass
morbido ≠ morbid MOHR-bee-doh	*morbido* = soft
notizia ≠ notice noh-TEETS-ee-yah	*notizia* = news
novella ≠ novel noh-VEHL-lah	*novella* = short story
parente ≠ parent pah-REHN-tay	*parente* = relative
patente ≠ patent pah-TEHN-tay	*patente* = driver's license
preservativo ≠ preservative preh-zehr-vah-TEE-voh	*preservativo* = condom
romanza ≠ romance	*romanza* = novel

False Friends

roh-MAHN-zah	
stormo ≠ storm	*stormo* = flock
STOHR-moh	
tasto ≠ taste	*tasto* = key (on a keyboard)
TAHSS-toh	
vacanza ≠ vacancy	*vacanza* = vacation
vah-KAHN-zah	

Chapter 2

Introducing Yourself

This book provides you with ready-made sentences and expressions to help you navigate many different situations. However, it is still very important to know the basics of grammar. Understanding the mechanics of the sentences and phrases presented here will make them that much more meaningful for you and can certainly help you to understand better when people are speaking to you!

Verbs and Conjugation

The following sections will help you to formulate basic sentences and questions. You've already learned about articles and nouns. Verbs form the foundation of any language. Here you will learn the basics about the simple present tense and simple past tense.

Verbs in the Present Tense

Most all Italian verbs fall into one of three categories—first conjugation verbs, second conjugation verbs, and third conjugation verbs. In order to determine in which category a particular verb belongs, we must look at the infinitive form of the verb. The infinitive is the unconjugated form of the verb (to run, to eat, etc.). First conjugation verbs end in *–are*; second conjugation verbs end in *–ere*; and third conjugation verbs end in *–ire*. Some examples follow:

–are verbs (first conjugation)

affittare	ahf-feet-TAHR-ray	to rent
guidare	gwee-DAH-ray	to drive
parlare	pahr-LAH-ray	to speak

–ere verbs (second conjugation)

vedere	veh-DEH-ray	to see
ripetere	ree-PEH-teh-ray	to repeat
leggere	LEHJ-jeh-ray	to read

–*ire* verbs (third conjugation)

dormire	door-MEE-ray	to sleep
partire	pahr-TEE-ray	to leave
capire	cah-PEE-ray	to understand

The first step in conjugating a verb is to identify the subject—I, you, he, Marco, John and I, etc. With the correct subject pronoun, you can correctly conjugate the verb.

Subject Pronouns
The subject pronouns (also referred to as personal pronouns) are used to indicate the subject of a verb.

Singular		Plural	
io	I	*noi*	we
ee-oo		*noy*	
tu	you (informal)	*voi*	you (informal)
too		voy	
lui, lei	he, she	*loro*	they
loo-ee, lay		*law-roh*	
Lei	you (formal)	*Loro*	you (formal)
lay		*law-roh*	

The next step is to conjugate the verb so that it is in the same person as the subject.

–*Are* Verbs in the Present Tense
Almost all –*are* verbs are regular—that is, they follow a pattern of conjugation. Once you learn this pattern, conjugating most –*are* verbs is easy! To conjugate the first

conjugation verbs in the present tense, remove the *–are* ending and replace it with a different ending for each subject:

Singular	Plural
io parlo (I speak)	*noi parliamo* (we speak)
ee-oh PAHR-loh	noy pahr-lee-AHM-oh
tu parli (you speak)	*voi parlate* (you speak)
too PAHR-lee	voy pahr-LAH-tay
lui parla (he speaks)	*loro parlano* (they speak)
loo-ee PAHR-lah	law-roh PAHR-lah-noh
lei parla (she speaks)	
lay PAHR-lah	
Lei parla (you [formal] speak)	Loro parlano (you [formal] speak)
lay PAHR-lah	law-roh PAHR-lah-noh

The present tense in Italian can carry different meanings in English, depending on the context:

> *Io parlo italiano* can mean "I speak Italian," "I am speaking Italian," or "I do speak Italian."
> *Io non parlo italiano* can mean "I don't speak Italian" or "I am not speaking Italian."

The present tense in Italian can also be used to express an action that will take place in the future:

> *Stasera guardo la televisione.*
> I will watch TV this evening.

–Ere and –ire Verbs in the Present Tense

Second and third conjugation verbs are verbs whose infinitive forms end in *–ere* and *–ire*, respectively. You will notice from the conjugations below that *–ere* and *–ire* verbs differ from each other only in the *voi* forms.

scrivere SCREE-veh-ray	to write	*dormire* door-MEE-ray	to sleep
io scrivo ee-oh SCREE-voh	*noi scriviamo* noy scree-vee-AH-moh	*io dormo* ee-oh DOOR-moh	*noi dormiamo* noy door-mee-AH-moh
tu scrivi too SCREE-vee	*voi scrivete* voy scree-VEH-tay	*tu dormi* too DOOR-mee	*voi dormite* voy door-MEE-tay
lui scrive loo-ee SCREE-veh	*loro scrivono* law-roh SCREE-voh-noh	*lui dorme* loo-ee DOOR-meh	*loro dormono* law-roh DOOR-moh-noh
Lei scrive lay SCREE-veh	*Loro scrivono* law-roh SCREE-voh-noh	*Lei dorme* lay DOOR-meh	*Loro dormono* law-roh DOOR-moh-noh
		lei scrive lay SCREE-veh	*lei dorme* lay DOOR-meh

The Verbs *Essere* and *Avere*

Essere (to be) and *avere* (to have) are two of the most common verbs, but they both require irregular conjugations.

Essere: To Be

The verb *essere* (to be) is one of the most commonly used verbs in Italian. It is important to learn this verb inside and out, as you will hear it in almost every conversation you have!

In the present tense, it is conjugated as follows:

Singular		Plural	
io sono	I am	*noi siamo*	we are
ee-oh SOH-noh		noy see-YAH-moh	
tu sei	you (informal)	*voi siete*	you (informal)
too say	are	voy see-YEH-teh	are
lui è	he is	*loro sono*	they are
loo-ee eh		LAW-roh soh-noh	
lei è	she is		
lay eh			
Lei è	you (formal)	*Loro sono*	you (formal) are
lay eh	are	LAW-roh soh-noh	

It is common, but not required, to omit the subject pronoun in both spoken and written Italian:

I am American.
Io sono americano.
ee-oh SOH-noh ah-meh-ree-CAH-noh

I am American.
Sono americano.

Essere can be used to indicate provenance when followed by the preposition *di* + a place name:

We are from Philadelphia.
Siamo di Philadelphia.
see-YAH-moh dee fill-ah-DEHL-fee-yah

To find out where someone is from, ask the question:

Di dove sei? (informal)
dee DOH-veh say?

Di dov'è? (formal)
dee doh-VEH?

Essere can be used to indicate possession when followed by the preposition *di* + a noun or a proper name:

It's my wife's suitcase.
È la valigia di mia moglie.
eh lah vah-LEE-jah dee mee-ah MOHL-yay

It's Paul's.
È di Paul.   eh dee Paul

To find out to whom something belongs, ask the question:

Whose is it?
Di chi è?   dee key eh

Whose are they?
Di chi sono?   dee key SOH-noh

Avere: To Have

The verb *avere* (to have) is a commonly used verb in Italian. It is conjugated in the present tense as follows:

Singular		Plural	
io ho ee-oh oh	I have	*noi abbiamo* noy ahb-bee-YAH-moh	we have
tu hai too eye	you (informal) have	*voi avete* voi ah-VEH-tay	you (informal) have
lui ha loo-ee ah	he has	*loro hanno* LAW-roh AHN-noh	they have
lei ha lay ah	she has		
Lei ha lay ah	you (formal) have	*Loro hanno* LAW-roh AHN-noh	you (formal) have

Do you have cousins in Florida?
Hai cugini in Florida?
eye koo-JEE-nee een FLOH-ree-dah

I have two cousins in Florida.
Ho due cugini in Florida.
oh doo-ay koo-JEE-nee een FLOH-ree-dah

The Past Tense

In order to form the *passato prossimo*, it is important to have mastered the auxiliary verbs *avere* and *essere*. The second component of the *passato prossimo* conjugations is the past participle. In Italian the past participle is formed by replacing the –*are*, –*ere*, –*ire* of the infinitive with –*ato*, –*uto*, –*ito*, respectively.

-FACT

In Italian the *passato prossimo* is also a compound tense that is made up of two parts: an auxiliary verb (either *avere* or *essere*) and the past participle of the verb. The *passato prossimo* can have a few different meanings: *Io ho viaggiato in Italia* could translate as "I have traveled to Italy," "I traveled to Italy," or "I did travel to Italy," depending on the context.

Infinitive	Past Participle
mangiare	*mangiato*
mahn-JAH-ray	mahn-JAH-toh
vedere	*veduto*
veh-DEH-ray	ved-DOO-toh
partire	*partito*
pahr-TEE-ray	pahr-TEE-toh

For most Italian verbs (including transitive verbs—those that can take a direct object), the *passato prossimo* is formed with the auxiliary verb *avere* plus the past participle of the main verb. The auxiliary verb *essere* is used with most intransitive verbs (verbs that cannot take a direct object). When the auxiliary verb *essere* is used, the last letter of the past participle must agree in number and in gender with the subject of the verb.

The Past Tense of the Verb *Vedere* (to see)

ho veduto oh veh-DOO-toh	I saw; I have seen
hai veduto eye veh-DOO-toh	you saw; you have seen
ha veduto ah veh-DOO-toh	he/she saw; has seen
abbiamo veduto ahb-bee-YAH-moh veh-DOO-toh	we saw; we have seen
avete veduto ah-VEH-tay veh-DOO-toh	you saw; you have seen
hanno veduto AHN-noh veh-DOO-toh	they saw; they have seen

Some examples of the past tense using *essere*:

The girls have left.
Le ragazze sono partite.
leh rah-GAHTS-seh SOH-noh pahr-TEE-teh

The boys arrived late.
I ragazzi sono arrivati in ritardo.
ee rah-GAHTS-see SOH-noh ahr-ree-VAH-tee een ree-TAHR-doh

The children went to the museum.
I bambini sono andati al museo.
ee bahm-BEE-nee SOH-noh ahn-DAH-tee ahl moo-ZAY-oh

Forming a Sentence

Developing your communication skills will require an understanding of basic sentence structure in Italian. Bear in mind that the following guidelines are not carved in stone; you will hear many variations in sentence structure based on context. These basic rules will help get you started.

1. Affirmative statement: *Paolo mangia la pizza.*
   (POWH-loh MAHN-jah lah PEETS-ah)
2. Negative statement: *Paolo non mangia la pizza.*
   (POWH-loh nohn MAHN-jah lah PEETS-ah)
3. Question: *Paolo mangia la pizza?*
   (POWH-loh MAHN-jah lah PEETS-ah?)

The basic structure of an affirmative statement in Italian is subject+verb+object. Making sentences negative in Italian is as easy as placing the word *non* in front of the conjugated verb.

Paul and Virginia are not from Boston.
Paul e Virginia non sono di Boston.
Paul eh Virginia nohn SOH-noh dee Boston

There are some two-part negative adverbs:

non . . . ancora	not yet
nohn ahn-KOH-rah	
non . . . mai	never
nohn meye	
non . . . più	no longer

nohn pyou
I've never traveled by train.
Non ho mai viaggiato in treno.
nohn oh meye vee-yah-JAH-toh een tray-noh

I am no longer working.
Non lavoro più.   nohn lah-VOH-roh PYOU

Asking a question in Italian is as easy as raising the pitch of your voice at the end of any sentence:

Are you American?
Tu sei americano?   too say ah-meh-ree-KAH-noh

Adjectives

An adjective is a word that describes or modifies a noun (an *interesting* book, an *American* businessman). In English, all adjectives come before the noun that they describe. This is not the case in Italian. In Italian, most adjectives follow the noun that they modify, but there is a category of commonly used adjectives that precede the nouns. Also, remember that, as we learned in Chapter 1, nouns have a number (singular or plural) and a gender (masculine or feminine). Italian adjectives must agree in gender and number with the nouns that they modify. That is, if a noun is masculine plural (*fratelli* [brothers], for example), the adjective that modifies it must be masculine and plural as well (*fratelli maggiori* [older brothers]). This means that there can be up to four forms of each adjective: masculine singular, feminine singular, masculine plural, and feminine plural.

Possessive, Demonstrative, and Interrogative Adjectives

Possessive, demonstrative, and interrogative adjectives all precede the nouns they modify.

- Possessive adjectives: *il mio, il tuo, il suo,* etc.
- Demonstrative adjectives: *questo* (this)
  questi (these), etc.
- Interrogative adjectives: *quale* (which)

Adjectives That Precede the Noun

Almost all adjectives follow the noun that they modify, but there are exceptions to that rule. The following is a group of commonly used adjectives that precede the noun they modify.

Italian adjective		English equivalent
altro	AHL-troh	other
bello	BEHL-loh	beautiful
bravo	BRAH-voh	good, able
brutto	BROOT-toh	ugly
buono	bwoo-OH-noh	good
caro	KAH-roh	dear; expensive
cattivo	kaht-TEE-voh	bad
giovane	JOH-vah-nay	young
grande	GRAHN-day	large; great
lungo	LOON-goh	long
nuovo	NWOH-voh	new
piccolo	PEEK-koh-loh	small, little
stesso	stehss-soh	same
vecchio	VEHK-kee-yo	old
vero	VEH-roh	true

When the adjective ends in –*e*, there is no difference between the masculine and feminine forms: *un ragazzo intelligente, una ragazza intelligente.*

-FACT

In some cases, an adjective can come either before or after the noun it modifies. In these cases the meaning of the adjective carries a subtle change in meaning. For example, *un vecchio amico* = an old friend (a friend I've known for a while), but *un amico vecchio* = an old friend (a friend who is elderly).

Some Useful Adjectives for Describing Yourself

Almost all adjectives follow the noun that they modify. The following is a group of commonly used adjectives that follow this rule:

Italian adjective		English equivalent
biondo	BYOHN-doh	blonde
bruno	BROO-noh	dark-haired
alto	AHL-toh	tall
basso	BAHSS-soh	short
snello	SNEHL-loh	slender
grasso	GRAHSS-soh	fat
giovane	JOH-vah-nay	young
vecchio	VEHK-kee-yo	old

Italian adjective		English equivalent
brutto	BROO-toh	ugly
ricco	REEK-koh	rich
povero	POH-veh-roh	poor
buono	bwoo-OH-noh	good
cattivo	kaht-TEE-voh	bad
intelligente	een-tehl-lee-JEHN-tay	intelligent
stupido	STOO-pee-doh	stupid
pigro	PEE-groh	lazy
simpatico	seem-PAH-tee-koh	kind
antipatico	ahn-tee-PAH-tee-koh	unpleasant
generoso	jehn-ehr-OHS-oh	generous
avaro	ah-VAH-roh	greedy
noioso	noy-OHS-oh	boring
felice	feh-LEE-cheh	happy
triste	TREESS-teh	sad

Adverbs

An adverb is a word that is used to modify a verb, an adjective, or an adverb. Adverbs are invariable; that is, they have only one form. Adverbs are used in a sentence to indicate manner, time, place, cause, or degree and to answer questions such as how, when, where, or how much. The placement of the adverb in Italian can be tricky, but the general rule states that when an adjective is modifying a verb, it should be placed after the verb: *Mangio volentieri in quel ristorante.* (I will gladly eat in that restaurant.) When the adverb modifies an adjective, it is placed in front of that adjective: *Maria è molto coraggiosa.* (Maria is very courageous.)

Prepositions

A preposition is a word that generally precedes a noun or pronoun and links it to another word in the sentence. Prepositions can have a variety of functions in a sentence:

- Direction: He's going *to* the store.
- Location: It's *in* the cabinet.
- Time: She arrived *after* the game ended.
- Possession: the United States *of* America

Here are some common Italian prepositions:

di (d')	dee	of, from
a	ah	at, to, in
da	dah	from, by
in	een	in
con	kohn	with
su	soo	on
per	pehr	for
tra, fra	trah, frah	between
verso	VEHR-soh	toward
tranne	TRAHN-neh	except
senza	SEHNZ-ah	without
sotto	SOHT-toh	under
oltre	OHL-treh	beside
sopra	SOH-prah	above
dietro	dee-AY-troh	behind
prima	PREE-mah	before
davanti	dah-VAHN-tee	in front

-FACT

> The prespositions *fra* and *tra* both mean between
> or among, and they can be used interchangeably.
> Depending on where you are in Italy, you may
> hear one over the other, but they are both univer-
> sally known and accepted as correct.

Articulated Prepositions

The prepositions *a*, *da*, *di*, *in*, and *su*, when used with
a definite article, combine with the definite article to form
one word. These are often referred to as prepositional articles, contractions, or articulated prepositions.

> *Vado a+il negozio = Vado al negozio.* I am going to
> the store.
> *Sono i bagagli di+gli studenti = Sono i bagagli degli
> studenti.* They are the students' suitcases.

	il	lo	l'(m.)	la	l'(f.)	i	gli	le
a	*al*	*allo*	*all'*	*alla*	*all'*	*ai*	*agli*	*alle*
	ahl	AHL-loh	ahll	AHL-lah	ahll	eye	AHL-yee	ahl-leh
di	*del*	*dello*	*dell'*	*della*	*dell'*	*dei*	*degli*	*delle*
	dehl	DEHL-loh	dehll	DEHL-lah	dehll	day	DEHL-yee	DEHL-leh
da	*dal*	*dallo*	*dall'*	*dalla*	*dall'*	*dai*	*dagli*	*dalle*
	dahl	DAHL-loh	dahll	DAHL-lah	dahll	deye	DAHL-yee	dahl-leh
su	*sul*	*sullo*	*sull'*	*sulla*	*sull'*	*sui*	*sugli*	*sulle*
	sool	SOOL-loh	sooll	SOOL-lah	sooll	SOO-ee	SOOL-yee	SOOL-leh
in	*nel*	*nello*	*nell'*	*nella*	*nell'*	*nei*	*negli*	*nelle*
	nehl	NEHL-loh	nehll	NEHL-lah	nehll	nay	NEHL-yee	NEHL-leh

Mastering Pronouns

Pronouns are words that substitute for nouns. There are many different types of pronouns, and mastering them can take time and effort. You've already learned about subject pronouns in Chapter 1; in this chapter we will have a look at direct object, indirect object, reflexive, and relative pronouns, all of which are very useful tools in developing a mastery of the language.

Direct Object Pronouns

A direct object pronoun is used to avoid unnecessary repetition of words in a sentence. Take a look at the following conversation:

Are you reading the newspaper?
No, I am not reading the newspaper.
Do you know if Mary is reading the newspaper?
No, I don't know if Mary is reading the newspaper.

The repetition of the direct object (newspaper) sounds rather strange to a native speaker of English. In order to avoid this unnecessary repetition, we can use the pronoun "it" in place of the direct object. The following conversation will sound better:

Are you reading the newspaper?
No, I'm not reading it.
Do you know if Mary is reading it?
No, I don't know if Mary is reading it.

-FACT

> In some cases, knowing which pronoun to use is a
> bit more complicated in Italian than it is in English.
> The equivalent of "it" can be either *lo* (used for a
> masculine singular direct object) or *la* (used for a
> feminine singular direct object in Italian); the pro-
> nouns *li* (masculine plural) and *le* (feminine plural)
> are used to mean "them."

Direct object pronouns are used the same way in
Italian. In Italian the forms of the direct object pronouns
(*i pronomi diretti*) are as follows:

Singular	Plural	
mi me	*ci*	us
mee	chee	
ti you (informal)	*vi* you (informal)	
tee	vee	
La you	*Li* you (formal, m.)	
(formal, m. and f.)	*Le* you (formal, f.)	
lah	lee / leh	
lo him, it	*li* them (m. and f.)	
loh	lee	
la her, it	*le* them (f.)	
lah	leh	

A direct object pronoun is placed immediately before
a conjugated verb.

> *Leggo il giornale* (LEHG-goh eel johr-NAH-lay)
>   becomes *Lo leggo* (loh LEHG-goh). ("I read the
>   newspaper" becomes "I read it.")
> *Compro la frutta* (KOHM-proh lah FROO-tah)
>   becomes *La compro* (lah KOHM-proh). ("I buy
>   the fruit" becomes "I buy it.")

In a negative sentence, the word *non* must come before the object pronoun.

> He doesn't eat it.
> *Non **la** mangia.*
> nohn lah MAHN-jah.

> Why don't you invite them?
> *Perché non **li** inviti?*
> pehr-KAY nohn lee een VEE-tee

Note that *mi, ti, lo-* and *la* change to *m', t',* and *l'* in front of a vowel or silent *h*.

Indirect Object Pronouns

The direct object in a sentence answers the question *what?* or *whom?* in relation to the verb. The indirect object nouns and pronouns answer the question *to whom?* or *for whom?* in relation to the verb. In English, the word "to" is often omitted: "We gave Paul a watch," instead of "We gave a watch to Paul." In Italian, the preposition *a* is always used before an indirect object noun. It goes without saying that if an article precedes the noun, then we must use an articulated preposition.

Indirect object pronouns (*i pronomi indiretti*) replace indirect object nouns. They are identical in form to direct object pronouns, except for the third person forms *gli*, *le*, and *loro*.

Singular	Plural
mi (to/for) me	*ci* (to/for) us
mee	chee
ti (to/for) you	*vi* (to/for) you
tee	vee
Le (to/for) you	*Loro* (to/for) you
(formal m. and f.)	(formal, m. and f.)
leh	LAW-roh
gli (to/for) him	*loro* (to/for) them
lyee (like *ll* sound in the	LAW-roh
English word *million*)	
le (to/for) her	
leh	

Indirect object pronouns, like direct object pronouns, precede a conjugated verb, except for *loro* and *Loro*, which always follow the verb.

I'm giving her the keys.
Le *do le chiavi.*
leh doh leh kee-YAH-vee

They offer us an aperitif.
Ci *offrono un aperitivo.*
chee OHF-froh-noh oon ah-peh-ree-TEE-voh

We'll talk to them this evening.
*Parliamo **loro** stasera.*
pahr-lee-YAH-moh LAW-roh stah-SAY-rah

I'm giving him a watch.
***Gli** regalo un orologio.*
lyee reh-GAH-loh oon oh-roh-LOH-joe

Note that *mi* and *ti* change to *m'* and *t'* in front of a vowel or silent *h*.

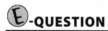-QUESTION

Should I use an indirect object pronoun or a direct object pronoun?
If the object is preceded by a preposition, that person/thing is an indirect object. If it is not preceded by a preposition, it is a direct object.

Reflexive Pronouns

Reflexive pronouns are used with reflexive verbs, which are verbs whose action falls back on the subject. Take a look at these sentences containing reflexive verbs:

I see myself in the mirror.
They enjoy themselves at the party.

In reflexive sentences, Italian verbs, like English verbs, are conjugated with reflexive pronouns. Reflexive pronouns (*i pronomi riflessivi*) are identical in form to direct object pronouns, except for the third person form *si* (the third-person singular and plural form).

Singular		Plural	
mi	myself	*ci*	ourselves
mee		chee	
ti	yourself	*vi*	yourselves
tee		vee	
si	himself, herself, itself,	*si*	themselves,
see	yourself (formal)	see	yourselves (formal)

Just like direct object pronouns, reflexive pronouns are placed before a conjugated verb.

> ***Mi** chiamo Michael* (mee KYAH-moh Michael).
> My name is Michael. (Literally, "I call myself Michael.")

Mi, *ti*, *si*, and *vi* may become *m'*, *t'*, *s'*, and *v'* before a vowel or silent *h*. *Ci* may only become *c'* before an *i* or *e*.

> She washes **herself** every day.
> *Maria **si** lava tutti i giorni.*
> mah-REE-ah see LAH-vah TOOT-tee ee JOHR-nee.

> We enjoy **ourselves** a lot.
> ***Ci** divertiamo molto.*
> chee dee-vehr-TYAH-moh MOHL-toh.

Reflexive verbs often have to do with parts of the body or clothing. You can recognize reflexive verbs by the *si* (oneself) attached to the infinitive. Here are some common reflexive verbs:

addormentarsi ahd-dohr-mehn-TAHR-see	to fall asleep
alzarsi ahl-ZAHR-see	to get up
annoiarsi ahn-noy-AHR-see	to get bored
arrabbiarsi ahr-rahb-BYAHR-see	to get angry
chiamarsi kyah-MAHR-see	to be called
divertirsi dee-vehr-TEER-see	to enjoy oneself
fermarsi fehr-MAHR-see	to stop (oneself)
innamorarsi een-nah-mohr-AHR-see	to fall in love
lavarsi lah-VAHR-see	to wash (oneself)
prepararsi preh-pahr-AHR-see	to get ready
riposarsi ree-poh-ZAHR-see	to relax
sposarsi spoh-ZAHR-see	to get married
sentirsi sehn-TEER-see	to feel
svegliarsi svel-YAHR-see	to wake up
vestirsi vehs-TEER-see	to get dressed

Chapter 3

Essential Italian

Chapter 3 outlines vocabulary and expressions that will prove useful to travelers. Apart from the ubiquitous phrases like "Do you speak English?" and "Where are you from?," this chapter discusses the differences between formal and informal speech, as well as numbers, days of the week, the calendar, and instructions for telling time.

Survival Italian

Take a look at the following Italian phrases—they might come in handy as you begin communicating.

I don't speak much Italian.
Non parlo bene l'italiano.
nohn PAHR-loh BEH-neh lee-tah-LYAH-noh

Repeat, please.
Ripeta, per favore.
REE-peh-tah peer fah-VOR-ay

Can you speak more slowly?
Può parlare più piano?
pwoh par-LAH-ray pyou PYAH-no

I don't understand.
Non capisco.
non kah-PEESS-koh

Do you speak English? (informal)
Parli inglese?
PAHR-lee een-GLEH-zhe

Do you speak English? (formal)
Parla inglese?
PAHR-lah een-GLEH-zhe

What does . . . mean?
Che cosa vuol dire . . . ?
keh coh-sah vwohl DEE-reh

How do you say . . . in Italian?
Come si dice . . . in italiano?
KOH-meh see DEE-cheh . . . in ee-tah-LYAH-noh

Language Basics

The following vocabulary forms the foundation of any conversation. Learning how to say yes and no and the valuable question words—who, what, when, where, and why—will help get any conversation started!

yes	*sì*	no	*no*
	see		noh
okay	*d'accordo*	and	*e*
	dah-KOHR-doh		eh
or	*o*	who	*chi*
	oh		kee
what	*che*	when	*quando*
	keh		KWAHN-doh
where	*dove*	why	*perché*
	DOH-veh		pehr-KEH
how	*come*		
	KOH-meh		

Being Polite

You'll notice that Italian verbs have both formal (*Lei*) and informal (*tu*) conjugations. Native speakers of English may find it difficult to gauge when the formal way of speaking should be used. As a general rule, the formal way of speaking should be used when meeting people for the first time, when greeting elders, and in business situations.

Italians may tell you when it's time to use the informal by saying *Diamoci del tu*, which means "Let's address each other informally." In any event, when you're not sure which to use, it's always safe to go with the formal. Though this may be too much to learn for the casual traveler, the following "polite" words can go a long way!

please	*per favore/per piacere/per cortesia*
	pehr FAHV-ohr-eh/pehr pyah-CHAY-reh/pehr cohr-teh-ZEE-ah
Thank you.	*Grazie.*
	GRAH-tsee-ay
Thank you very much.	*Mille grazie.*
	MEEL-leh GRAH-tsee-ay
You're welcome.	*Prego.*
	PRAY-goh
It's my pleasure.	*Piacere mio.*
	pyah-CHAY-reh MEE-oh
Pardon me.	*Mi scusi.*
	mee SCOO-zee
I'm sorry.	*Mi dispiace.*
	mee dees-PYAH-chay

Titles (capitalized before a name)

sir, Mr.	*signore*
	seen-YOHR-ay
ma'am, Mrs.	*signora*
	seen-YOHR-ah
miss	*signorina*
	seen-YOHR-ee-nah

Numbers 1 Through 100 and Beyond

How many bottles of wine should you order? How much bread should you buy? Learning the numbers will help you communicate these decisions!

Numbers 1 to 100

1	*uno*	OO-noh
2	*due*	DOO-ay
3	*tre*	tray
4	*quattro*	KWAHT-troh
5	*cinque*	CHIN-kway
6	*sei*	say
7	*sette*	SET-tay
8	*otto*	OHT-toh
9	*nove*	NOH-vay
10	*dieci*	DYEH-chee
11	*undici*	OON-dee-chee
12	*dodici*	DOH-dee-chee
13	*trédici*	TREH-dee-chee
14	*quattordici*	kwaht-TOHR-dee-chee
15	*quindici*	KWEEN-dee-chee
16	*sedici*	SAY-dee-chee
17	*diciassette*	dee-chah-SEHT-tay
18	*diciotto*	dee-CHOHT-toh
19	*diciannove*	dee-chah-NOH-vay
20	*venti*	VEHN-tee
21	*ventuno*	vehn-TUH-noh
22	*ventidue*	vehn-tee-DOO-eh
23	*ventitré*	vehn-tee-TREH
24	*ventiquattro*	vehn-tee-KWAHT-troh
25	*venticinque*	vehn-tee-CHIN-kweh

26	*ventisei*	vehn-tee-SAY
27	*ventisette*	vehn-tee-SEHT-teh
28	*ventotto*	vehn-TOHT-toh
29	*ventinove*	vehn-tee-NOHV-vay
30	*trenta*	TREHN-tah
40	*quaranta*	kwah-RAHN-tah
50	*cinquanta*	chin-KWAHN-tah
60	*sessanta*	sess-AHN-tah
70	*settanta*	seht-TAHN-tah
80	*ottanta*	oht-TAHN-tah
90	*novanta*	nohv-AHN-tah
100	*cento*	CHEHN-toh

The numbers *venti*, *trenta*, *quaranta*, up to *novanta* drop the final vowel before adding *uno* and *otto*. *Tre* takes on an accent mark when it is added to *venti*, *trenta*, and so on.

-SSENTIAL

All numbers are invariable except *uno*. *Uno*, you may notice, has the same forms as the indefinite article (*un*, *uno*, *una*, *un'*) when it comes before a noun. *Un telefonino* could mean "a cell phone" or "one cell phone," depending on the context.

Larger Numbers

1,000	*mille*
	MEEHL-leh
1,200	*milleduecento*
	meehl-leh-doo-ay-CHEN-toh

2,000	*duemila*
	doo-ay-MEE-lah
5,000	*cinquemila*
	chin-kway-MEE-lah
10,000	*diecimila*
	dyeh-chee-MEE-lah
100,000	*centomila*
	chen-toh-MEE-lah
1,000,000	*un milione*
	oon mil-LYOH-neh
1,000,000,000	*un miliardo*
	oon meel-YAHR-doh

-FACT

Writing out numerals in Italian can be tricky. Italians use a decimal point where a comma would be used in the United States, and vice versa. So the (American) 1,200 would be written as 1.200 in Italy, and the American 1.5 (as in one and a half) would be written as 1,5 in Italy.

Che ora è? Che ore sono?: Telling Time in Italian

You have a flight at 15.00 and you have to get to the bank before it closes at 13.00. Telling time in Italian differs from telling time in English. Italians use military time to track the hours of the day, and they use a period where a colon would be used in English. It can be tricky, but the following guide will save you from missing your important appointments!

The questions *Che ora è?* and *Che ore sono?* both mean "What time is it?" and can be used interchangeably.

What time is it?	*Che ora è?* keh OHR-ah EH
What time is it?	*Che ore sono?* keh OHR-eh SOH-noh
It's 8:30.	*Sono le otto e trenta.* soh-noh leh OHT-toh eh TREHN-tah

The expression *È l'* . . . is used to express all times using the 1:00 hour.

It's 1:00.	*È l'una.* eh LOO-nah
It's 1:10.	*È l'una e dieci.* eh LOO-nah eh DYEH-chee
It's 12:55. (It's 1:00 minus 5.)	*È l'una meno cinque.* eh LOO-nah MAY-noh CHIN-kway
It's 1:45.	*È l'una e quarantacinque.* eh LOO-nah eh kwah-rahn-tah CHIN-kway

And *È* . . . is used with the following time expressions:

It's noon.	*È mezzogiorno.* eh mehts-oh JOHR-noh
It's midnight.	*È mezzanotte.* eh mehts-ah NOHT-tay

The expression *Sono le . . .* is used to express all times from 2:00 on:

It's 12:20.	*Sono le dodici e venti.* soh-noh leh DOH-dee-chee eh VEHN-tee
It's 2:00.	*Sono le due.* soh-noh leh DOO-ay
It's 3:15.	*Sono le tre e quindici.* soh-noh leh treh e KWEEN-dee-chee
It's 4:30.	*Sono le quattro e mezzo.* soh-noh leh KWAHT-troh a MEHD-soh
It's 4:42.	*Sono le quattro e quarantadue.* soh-noh leh KWAHT-troh eh kwah-rahn-tah-DOO-ay
It's 5:05.	*Sono le cinque e cinque.* soh-noh leh CHIN-kway e CHIN-kway
It's 6:55.	*Sono le sette meno cinque* or *Sono le sei e cinquantacinque.* soh-noh leh SEHT-teh MAY-noh CHIN-kway or soh-noh leh say eh chin-kwahn-tah-CHIN-kway
It's 7:58. (It's 8:00 minus 2.)	*Sono le otto meno due.* soh-noh leh OHT-toh MAY-noh DOO-ay
It's 8 A.M.	*Sono le otto di mattina.* soh-noh leh OHT-toh dee maht-TEE-nah
It's 10 P.M.	*Sono le dieci di sera.* soh-noh leh DYEH-chee dee say-rah

-FACT

In Italy, it's common to see the twenty-four-hour clock used for scheduling purposes. Expect to see it when you look at train or plane schedules, conference schedules, television programming, and so on.

The Calendar

The Italian calendar begins with Monday and ends with the weekend (logical, no?) days Saturday and Sunday. Days of the week, months of the year, and names of seasons are not capitalized in Italian unless, of course, they are at the beginning of the sentence.

Days of the Week

Monday	*lunedì*	loo-neh-DEE
Tuesday	*martedì*	mahr-teh-DEE
Wednesday	*mercoledì*	mehr-coh-leh-DEE
Thursday	*giovedì*	joh-veh-DEE
Friday	*venerdì*	vehn-ehr-DEE
Saturday	*sabato*	SAH-bah-toh
Sunday	*domenica*	doh-MEH-nee-kah

The days of the workweek are related to the names of the planets: *lunedì*, the day of the Moon (*Luna*); *martedì*, the day of Mars (*Marte*); *mercoledì*, the day of Mercury (*Mercurio*); *giovedì*, the day of Jupiter (*Giove*); *venerdì*, the day of Venus (*Venere*). The word for Saturday (*sabato*) is related to the word for Sabbath, and the word for Sunday (*domenica*), is related to the Latin words *Dominicus* and *Dominus*, which have a religious significance, referring to God.

Months of the Year

January	*gennaio*	jehn-NAHY-oh
February	*febbraio*	fehb-BRAHY-oh
March	*marzo*	MARTS-oh
April	*aprile*	ahp-REE-leh
May	*maggio*	MAHJ-joh
June	*giugno*	JOON-yoh
July	*luglio*	LOOL-yoh
August	*agosto*	ah-GOHS-toh
September	*settembre*	seht-TEHM-breh
October	*ottobre*	oht-TOH-breh
November	*novembre*	nohv-EHM-breh
December	*dicembre*	dee-CHEM-breh

You may notice that the months *settembre*, *ottobre*, *novembre*, and *dicembre* look similar to the words for seven (*sette*), eight (*otto*), nine (*nove*), and ten (*dieci*). This may lead one to conclude that *settembre* (September) is the seventh month, *ottobre* (October) is the eighth, *novembre* (November) is the ninth, and *dicembre* (December) is the tenth, which is obviously not the case in modern times. This interesting phenomenon has its roots in the Roman calendar, which began in March so that September, October, November, and December were the seventh, eighth, ninth, and tenth months of the Roman year.

Seasons

spring	*la primavera*	lah pree-mah-VEHR-ah
summer	*l'estate*	less-TAH-teh
autumn	*l'autunno*	lahw-TOO-noh
winter	*l'inverno*	leen-VEHR-noh

Exchanging Money

Many tourists may be used to the old and faithful traveler's checks. This chapter will help shed some light on other, more convenient, and perhaps easier ways of getting your hands on some euros while you vacation in Italy.

ATMs are Called *Bancomat*

Buying euros from your bank in the United States can be expensive. Most banks will charge up to 10 percent in fees. The same goes for exchanging money at exchange counters in airports and hotels in Italy. The best exchange rates can be found at ATMs (*bancomat*, pronounced BAHN-koh-maht). Check with your bank before you leave to determine if there are any service charges involved with ATM use abroad. Your bank may allow free ATM use through a specific Italian network (Cirrus or BankMate are two of the most widely available). ATMs in Italy will usually only allow you to withdraw money from your primary account (usually your checking account). If you're used to keeping a low balance in your checking account and a high balance in savings, you may want to call your bank to make sure that your checking and savings accounts are linked.

-FACT

The keypad of an Italian ATM is made up of numbers only, so make sure you memorize the numerical equivalent of your password.

Banks

If you do not have an ATM card, your best bet is to exchange money at a bank. Be advised, though—banks in Italy have limited hours. They are usually open from 8:30 A.M. to 1:30 P.M., and again from 3:00 P.M. to 4:00 or 5:00 P.M. Paperwork can take some time, and the exchange rate, though it may be better than what you might find at the airport, still leaves a bit to be desired.

Credit Cards

Major credit card accounts usually offer cash advance type services. These transactions benefit from the anti-fraud protection that accompanies your account (save your receipts!). Though the exchange rates can be compatible, check on the types of fees and charges associated with these transactions. If you plan on using a credit card for purchases while you are in Italy, make sure to call your bank or credit card company before you leave to confirm that you will be using your card in Italy. Not doing so may alert your credit card company's anti-fraud department at an inopportune time!

Traveler's Checks

Many travelers still insist on the convenience and safety that traveler's checks offer. With the prominence of ATMs and credit card use, travelers will find that traveler's checks are not as widely accepted as they used to be. You will be able to exchange them in banks and in hotels, but don't count on them being accepted at local shops and restaurants.

The Euro

The euro is used as the national currency in twelve European countries, including Italy. The seven banknote denominations (5, 10, 20, 50, 100, 200, 500) have a common design in all countries, but the eight denominations of coins have a single European design on one side, and unique national designs on the other.

Coin	Design
1 cent	Castel del Monte in Apulia
2 cent	the Mole Antonelliana Tower in Torino
5 cent	the Colosseum in Rome
10 cent	Sandro Botticelli's *Birth of Venus*
20 cent	*Unique Forms of Continuity in Space* sculpture by Umberto Boccioni
50 cent	Statue of Emperor Marcus Aurelius on horseback
1 euro	Leonardo da Vinci's famous drawing of the human body
2 euro	drawing of Dante Alighieri by Raphael

Useful Vocabulary and Phrases

The following terms and expressions will help you navigate Italian financial institutions—or at least they will help you as you try to exchange money.

Money and the Bank

money	*il denaro/i soldi*
	eel deh-NAH-roh/ee SOHL-dee
the euro	*l'euro*
	leh-oo-roh
change	*il cambio*
	eel KAHM-bee-yoh
banknote	*la banconota*
	lah bahn-kah-NOH-tah
coin	*la moneta*
	lah moh-NEH-tah
currency	*la valuta*
	lah vah-LOO-tah
dollar	*il dollaro*
	eel DOHL-lah-roh
British pound sterling	*la sterlina*
	lah stehr-LEE-nah
check	*l'assegno*
	lahss-SEHN-yoh
traveler's check	*il travelers check*
	eel travelers check
to cash (a check)	*incassare un assegno*
	een-cahss-SAH-ray oon ahss-SEHN-yoh
bank	*la banca*
	lah BAHN-kah
counter	*lo sportello*
	loh spohr-TEHL-loh

teller window	*la cassa*
	lah CAHSS-sah
exchange rate	*il tasso di cambio*
	eel TAHSS-oh dee KAHM-bee-yoh
to sign	*firmare*
	feehr-MAH-ray

At the Bank

To which counter do I go to change money?
A che sportello devo andare per cambiare del denaro?
ah keh spohr-TEHL-loh DAY-voh ahn-DAH-ray pehr kahm-BYAH-ray dehl deh-NAH-roh

Is there a commission?
C'è una commissione da pagare?
cheh oo-nah kohm-mees-YOH-nay dah pah-GAH-ray

What's the exchange rate for the dollar?
Qual'è il tasso di cambio per il dollaro?
kwahl eh eel TAHSS-soh dee KAHM-bee-yoh pehr eel DOHL-lah-roh

Where do I have to sign?
Dove devo firmare?
DOH-veh DAY-voh feehr-MAH-ray

What is today's date?
Qual'è la data di oggi?
kwahl eh lah DAH-tah dee ohj-jee

What time does the bank open?
A che ora apre la banca?
ah keh oh-rah AH-preh lah BAHN-kah

What time does the bank close?
A che ora chiude la banca?
ah keh oh-rah KYOO-deh lah BAHN-kah

Do you accept credit cards?
Accettate la carta di credito?
ah-cheht-TAH-tay lah KAHR-tah dee CREH-dee-toh

Can you change money for me?
Potete cambiare delle banconote per me?
poh-TEH-teh kahm-BYAH-ray dehl-leh bahn-kah-
NOHT-tay pehr meh

Can you change dollars for me?
Potete cambiare dei dollari per me?
poh-TEH-teh kahm-BYAH-ray day DOHL-lah-ree pehr
meh

Can you change American/Australian/Canadian dollars for me?
*Potete cambiare dei dollari Americani/Australiani/
Canadesi per me?*
poh-TEH-teh kahm-BYAH-ray day DOHL-lah-ree ah-
meh-ree-KAH-nee/ous-strahl-YAH-nee/kah-nah-
DAY-zee pehr meh

Where can I get money changed?
Dove posso cambiare delle banconote?
DOH-veh POHSS-soh kahm-BYAH-ray dehl-leh bahn-
  kah-NOHT-tay

Where can I get foreign money changed?
Dove posso cambiare della valuta straniera?
DOH-veh POHSS-soh kahm-BYAH-ray dehl-lah vah-
  LOO-tah strahn-YEH-rah

Where can I change a traveler's check?
Dove posso cambiare un travelers check?
DOH-veh POHSS-soh kahm-BYAH-ray oon travelers
  check

What is today's exchange rate?
Quant' è il cambio di oggi?
kwahn-TEH eel KAHM-byoh dee ohj-jee

Where is an automatic teller machine (ATM)?
Dove posso trovare un Bancomat?
DOH-veh pohss-soh troh-VAH-ray oon BAHN-koh-
  maht

Chapter 4

Meeting People

Making an effort to greet people in their native language is one way to show respect. This chapter introduces you to some basic ice breakers—adjectives and expressions that you can use to start conversations and describe yourself. You'll recognize several verbs in the present tense, as well as some nouns, articles, adjectives, and pronouns thrown in for good measure. This chapter will also give you some pointers on making telephone calls in Italy.

Greetings

This section introduces you to some valuable expressions that you can use to greet people and start a conversation. Remember, when introducing yourself, be confident and polite!

Ice Breakers

These are the essentials.

Good morning.
Buona mattina.
BWOHN-ah mah-TEE-na

Good day.
Buon giorno.
bwohn JOHR-no

Good evening.
Buona sera.
BWOHN-ah SAY-ra

Goodnight.
Buona notte.
BWOHN-ah NOHT-tay

Hello! (formal)
Salve!
SAHL-vay

Hi! (informal)
Ciao!
chow

-**ALERT**

Many of us are familiar with the word *ciao*. It does indeed mean both hello and goodbye, but it is considered to be very informal. You would use it with friends, but be careful using it in other, more formal, situations. You would not use it, for example, in a formal business meeting when addressing potential business partners.

Conversation Starters

Once you get past the greetings, you may want to get the conversation rolling. Here are some useful conversation starters.

How are you?	*Come stai?*
	KOH-meh sty
Fine, thanks.	*Bene, grazie.*
	BEH-neh, GROTS-ee-eh
Excellent!	*Ottimo!*
	OHT-tee-moh
Yes.	*Sì.*
	see
No.	*No.*
	noh
My name is . . .	*Mi chiamo . . .*
	mee KYAH-moh
What's your name? (formal)	*Come si chiama Lei?*
	KOH-meh see KYAH-mah lay

What's your name? (informal)	*Come ti chiami?* KOH-meh tee KYAH-mee too
His name is . . .	*Lui si chiama . . .* loo-ee see KYAH-mah . . .
Her name is . . .	*Lei si chiama . . .* lay see KYAH-mah
I am . . .	*Sono . . .* SOH-noh
Where are you from?	*Di dove sei?* dee DOH-veh say
I am from . . .	*Sono di . . .* SOH-noh dee
I come from . . .	*Vengo da. . .* VEN-goh dah
. . . the United States	*gli Stati Uniti* llyee STAH-tee you-NEE-tee
. . . England	*l'Inghilterra* lin-gill-TAY-rah
. . . Australia	*l'Australia* louse-TRAH-lyah (louse, pronounced like house)
. . . Canada	*la Canada* lah KAH-nah-dah
. . . France	*la Francia* lah FRAN-chah
. . . Spain	*la Spagna* lah SPAHN-yah
. . . China	*la Cina* lah CHEE-nah
. . . Japan	*il Giappone* eel jah-POH-nay
Thank you.	*Grazie.* GROTS-ee-eh

Please (Here you are).	*Prego.*
	PRAY-go
You're welcome.	*Non c'è di che.*
	nohn che dee keh
May I introduce you to . . . ?	*Posso presentarti . . . ?*
	POH-soh pre-zen-TAR-tee
Nice to meet you.	*Piacere di conoscerti.*
	pee-AHCH-air-ay dee
	koh-NOSH-ehr-tee
Bye!	*Arrivederci.*
	ah-ree-vehr-DEHR-chee
Goodbye (for good).	*Addio.*
	AHD-dee-o
See you . . .	*Ci vediamo . . .*
	chee-vehd-YAH-moh
. . . tomorrow.	*. . . domani.*
	doh-MAH-nee
. . . this afternoon.	*. . . questo pomeriggio.*
	KWES-toh pohm-her-REEJ-ee-oh
. . . this evening.	*. . . stasera.*
	stah-SAY-rah
. . . next week.	*. . . la settimana prossima.*
	lah seht-tee-MAH-nah
	prohs-SEE-mah
. . . in an hour.	*. . . tra un'ora.*
	trah oon OHR-ah
. . . later.	*. . . piu'tardi.*
	pyoo TAHR-dee
Do you speak . . . (informal)	*Parli . . .*
	PAHR-lee
Do you speak . . . (formal)	*Parla . . .*
	PAHR-lah

... English?	... *inglese?*
	een-GLEH-zay
... German?	... *tedesco?*
	teh-DESS-Koh
... French?	... *francese?*
	frahn-CHEH-zay
... Spanish?	... *spagnolo?*
	spahn-YOH-loh
Where is ... ?/	*Dov'è. . . ?/Dove sono. . . ?*
Where are ... ?	dohv-EH/DOH-veh SOH-noh
Can you tell me ... ?	*Puoi dirmi . . . ?*
(informal)	poo-oi DEER-mee
Can you tell me ... ?	*Può dirmi . . . ?*
(formal)	pwoh DEER-mee
Can you show me ... ?	*Puoi mostrarmi . . . ?*
(informal)	poo-oi mohs-TRAHR-mee
Can you show me ... ?	*Può mostrarmi . . . ?*
(formal)	pwoh mohs-TRAHR-mee

Nationalities and Languages

Italy is a tourist destination for travelers the world over. Whether you arrive at one of Italy's international airports or catch a train at one of Italy's numerous train stations, you can expect to meet travelers from just about any country in the world. Talking about where you are from and asking where other people are from is a good way to practice your Italian. The following is a list of adjectives in the masculine form; see Chapter 2 for an explanation of how to form the feminine and plural endings.

-FACT

Adjectives denoting nationality are not capitalized in Italian. "I am American" is *Sono americano*,
or *Sono americana*. Nouns denoting nationalities
are capitalized in Italian—*gli Italiani, gli Americani,
i Cinesi*, and so on.

I am ...	*Sono ... (SOH-noh ...)*
African	*africano* ah-free-KAH-noh
American	*americano* ah-meh-ree-KAH-no
Australian	*australiano* ouse-strahl-YAH-no
Belgian	*belgo* BEHL-goh
Brazilian	*brasiliano* brah-zeel-YAH-noh
Canadian	*canadese* kah-nah-DEH-say
Chinese	*cinese* chee-NEH-say
Dutch	*olandese* oh-lahn-DEH-say
English	*inglese* een-GLEH-say
Egyptian	*egiziano* eh-jits-YAH-noh
European	*europeo* eh-oo-roh-PEH-oh

French	*francese*
	frahn-CHEH-say
German	*tedesco*
	teh-DESS-koh
Indian	*indiano*
	een-dee-YAH-noh
Irish	*irlandese*
	eer-lahn-DAY-say
Italian	*italiano*
	ee-tahl-YAH-noh
Japanese	*giapponese*
	jahp-poh-NEH-say
Mexican	*messicano*
	meh-see-KAH-noh
Moroccan	*marocchino*
	mah-roh-KEE-noh
New Zealander	*neozelandese*
	nay-oh-zeh-lahn-DAY-say
Polish	*polacco*
	poh-LAHK-koh
Portuguese	*portoghese*
	pohr-toh-GAY-say
Russian	*russo*
	ROOS-soh
Scottish	*scozzese*
	skohts-ZAY-say
Spanish	*spagnolo*
	spahn-YOH-loh
Swedish	*svedese*
	sveh-DAY-say
Swiss	*svizzero*
	sveets-TSEH-roh

Family Members

After you've introduced yourself, a good way to continue the conversation is to talk about your family members.

father	*il padre (il papà)*
	eel PAH-dray, eel pah-PAH
mother	*la madre (la mamma)*
	lah MAH-dray, lah MAH-mah
parents	*i genitori*
	ee jehn-ee-TOHR-ee
brother	*il fratello*
	eel frah-TEHL-loh
sister	*la sorella*
	lah soh-REHL-lah
son	*il figlio*
	eel FEEL-yoh
daughter	*la figlia*
	lah FEEL-yah
grandfather	*il nonno*
	eel NOHN-noh
grandmother	*la nonna*
	lah NOHN-nah
grandparents	*i nonni*
	ee NOHN-nee
grandchildren	*i nipoti*
	ee nee-POH-tee
uncle	*lo zio*
	loh DSEE-oh
aunt	*la zia*
	lah DSEE-ah
nephew	*il nipote*
	eel nee-POH-tay

niece	*la nipote* lah nee-POH-tay
husband	*il marito* eel mah-REE-toh
wife	*la moglie* lah MOHL-yay
fiancé	*il fidanzato* eel fee-dahn-TSAH-toh
fiancée	*la fidanzata* lah fee-dahn-TSAH-tah
stepfather	*il patrigno* eel pah-TREEN-yoh
stepmother	*la matrigna* lah mah-TREEN-yah
cousin	*il cugino, la cugina* eel koo-JEEN-oh, lah koo-JEEN-ah
brother-in-law	*il cognato* eel kohn-YAH-toh
sister-in-law	*la cognata* lah kohn-YAH-tah
father-in-law	*il suocero* eel SWOH-cheh-roh
mother-in-law	*la suocera* lah SWOH-cheh-rah
child	*il bambino, la bambina* eel bahm-BEE-noh, lah bahm-BEE-nah
baby	*il bimbo, la bimba* eel BEEM-boh, lah BEEM-bah
married	*sposato* spoh-ZAH-toh
single	*celibe (m.), nubile (f.)* CHE-lee-bay, NOO-bee-lay

divorced	*divorziato(a)*
	dee-vohrts-YAH-toh (tah)
separated	*separato*
	seh-pah-RAH-toh
widowed	*vedovo*
	VEH-doh-voh

-FACT

> The words *il nipote* and *la nipote* can refer to either grandchild or niece/nephew. The context of the conversation can help to clarify. If you're still not sure, just ask!

Telephoning to and from Italy

From calling a hotel in Rome to calling a restaurant for a quiet table for two, this section will help you navigate the Italian telecommunications system.

Calling Italy from the United States and Canada

To place a call from the United States or Canada, first dial the United States international code 011, then dial Italy's country code 39, then dial the city code (06 for Rome, 055 for Florence), and finally dial the number, which can be six or seven digits. For example, if the Italian phone number in Rome is 55-55-55, you must dial the following: 011-39-06-55-55.

Calling Another Country from Italy

To place a call to another country from Italy, first dial the Europe long distance code 00, then the country code (1 for the United States and Canada), then the area code and number.

Country Codes of Other Countries

United States	1
Canada	1
United Kingdom	44
France	33
Germany	49
Spain	34
Switzerland	41

Placing a Call Within Italy

Italian phone numbers are comprised of an area code (this can be from two to four digits and begins with a zero) and the phone number. Cell phone area codes begin with the number 3, and area codes that begin with the number 8 are toll-free. To make a call from one area code to another, you must dial the full area code and number. To call within the same area code, you must dial the area code as well.

-ALERT

Remember, Italy is six hours ahead of the United States Eastern Standard Time (EST). For example, at midnight in Boston, it is 6:00 A.M. in Rome.

Public Phones

Public phones are easy to find. They're literally every-where, and most bars and coffee shops will have one on the premises. The phone booths are egg-shaped and are usually painted a bright orange color for easy recognition. You can pay for a public phone with coins (*monete*), with a phone card (*scheda telefonica*), or with a credit card (*carta di credito*). Some older phones will only take coins, and some of the newer phones will only take a phone or credit card.

Phone cards can be purchased from machines at the airport and train stations and at most tobacco stores and bars. They are available in various denominations. To use the phone card, you must first break off the perforated corner in the upper part of the card, which will allow the card to fit into the slot on the phone. Once you've inserted the card, it is activated.

You may come across public Internet Corners. They can be used with phone cards. These stations may not work very well, so do not depend on them for Internet access.

Emergency Numbers

In the rare instance that you need to get in touch with emergency services, here is how to reach them:

- **112:** Emergencies. Much like 911 in the United States, this is a European Union-wide emergency number with multilingual operators that can route your emer-gency to the appropriate agency.
- **113:** Emergencies (local police). *Polizia di stato*, national civilian police.

- **115:** Fire department.
- **117:** *Guardia di finanza* (financial police). If a business has cheated you, this is the number to call.
- **118:** Ambulance.

Cell Phones

We've become accustomed to the convenience of having a cell phone on our persons. Whether you plan on bringing your cell phone with you or buying (or renting) one while you're there, this section will give some valuable pointers.

GSM (Global System for Mobile Communications) is a type of cell phone and network that is used in most countries in the world, including Europe. Some U.S. cell phone service providers use GSM, but most do not. You will need a GSM phone in Italy. GSM phones are sometimes called world phones because they can be used around the world.

Check with your cell phone service provider to determine if yours is a GSM phone. If it is not, world phones can be purchased easily and inexpensively from numerous online vendors. If you have a GSM phone, check with your service provider to determine the costs involved with using your phone while you are abroad. Some companies offer reasonable rates for use abroad, while others are quite expensive.

If your U.S. cellular service provider does not offer international service, it is possible—and often economical—to rent a world phone complete with a SIM card from a reputable online source such as RangeRoamer (*www.rangeroamer.com*) or Call in Europe (*www.callineurope*

.com). Waiting until you arrive in Italy and renting a phone at the airport or from a cell phone store is possible but time-consuming.

SIM Cards

A SIM (Subscriber Information Module) card is a small chip inserted into your phone that contains your cell phone number and your account information. The SIM card can easily be switched from one phone to another. Provided you're in possession of a world phone, it may be possible for you to purchase a SIM card in Italy and simply use it while you travel. This is a good option all over Europe because cell phone plans in Europe do not require lengthy contract commitments. SIM cards come with a certain number of prepaid minutes; once you've used your minutes, you can either discard the SIM card or purchase more minutes. Also, there is no per-minute charge for incoming calls.

Telephone Vocabulary

cell phone	*telefonino/cellulare*
	teh-leh-foh-NEE-noh/chehl-loo-LAH-reh
reverse charges/	*a carico del destinatario*
collect call	ah KAH-ree-koh dehl
	des-tee-nah-TAH-ree-oh
busy	*occupato*
	ohk-koo-PAH-toh
please hold	*stia in linea*
	STEE-ah een LEE-nay-ah
to hang up	*riagganciare*
	ree-ah-gahn-CHAH-ray

to call back	*richiamare* ree-kyah-MAH-ray
to ring	*squillare* skwee-LAH-ray
telephone	*il telefono* eel teh-LEH-foh-noh
telephone booth	*la cabina telefonica* lah kah-BEE-nah teh-leh-FOH-nee-kah
telephone call	*la telefonata* lah teh-leh-foh-NAH-tah
telephone directory	*la guida telefonica* lah GWEE-dah teh-leh-FOH-nee-kah
telephone number	*il numero di telefono* eel NOO-meh-roh dee teh-LEH-foh-noh
dialing tone	*il segnale acustico* eel sehn-YAH-lay ah-KOO-stee-koh

Chapter 5

Airports, Trains, and Hotels

The previous chapters have provided you with the framework for basic conversation and the building blocks (verbs, adjectives, adverbs, and basic expressions) to expand your communicative ability. This chapter will build on that framework and will provide you with the very practical and useful information you need to navigate the airport, the train station, and the hotel.

The Verb *Volere*

The Italian verb *volere* means "to want."

I want to travel.
Voglio viaggiare.
vohl-yoh vee-ah-JAH-ray

I would like to travel.
Vorrei viaggiare.
vohr-ray vee-ah-JAH-ray

Volere is an irregular Italian verb. For the purposes of this book, it is presented here in its two most useful forms: the present indicative tense and the present conditional mood.

present		conditional	
voglio	vohl-yoh	*vorrei*	vohr-ray
vuoi	voo-oy	*vorresti*	vohr-REHS-tee
vuole	voo-OH-leh	*vorrebbe*	vohr-REHB-beh
vogliamo	vohl-YAH-moh	*vorremo*	vohr-REH-moh
volete	voh-LEH-teh	*vorreste*	voh-REHS-teh
vogliono	VOHL-yoh-noh	*vorrebbero*	vohr-REHB-beh-roh

In Italy it is more polite to express your desires and wishes with the present conditional mood.

I'd like a ticket.
Vorrei un biglietto.
voh-ray oon beel-YEH-toh

The Verbs *Andare* and *Venire*

These two verbs are also important for travelers to know. *Andare* means "to go" and *venire* means "to come." These two verbs are most useful in the present indicative tense and the *passato prossimo*.

> We are going to Rome.
> *Andiamo a Roma.*
> ahn-dee-YAH-moh ah roh-mah

> He's coming with us.
> *Lui viene con noi.*
> loo-ee vyeh-neh kohn noy

Present	*andare*	*venire*
io	*vado*	*vengo*
	vah-doh	vehn-goh
tu	*vai*	*vieni*
	veye (pronounced like the English word "eye")	vee-EH-nee
lui, lei, Lei	*va*	*viene*
	vah	vee-EH-neh
noi	*andiamo*	*veniamo*
	ahn-dee-AH-moh	veh-nee-YAH-moh
voi	*andate*	*venite*
	ahn-DAH-tay	veh-NEE-teh
loro, Loro	*vanno*	*vengono*
	vahn-noh	VEHN-goh-noh

Both *andare* and *venire* are conjugated with *essere* in the past tense (*passato prossimo*). Though *andare* has a regular past participle (*andato*), *venire* has a slightly irregular past participle (*venuto*).

-SSENTIAL

The verbs *andare* and *venire* are both irregular in the present tense. You will notice that several commonly used verbs have irregular conjugations.

Airport and Flight Vocabulary

The hustle and bustle of the airport can be stressful. The following terms and expressions may help to alleviate some of that stress.

People, Places, and Things

airplane	*un aereo*
	oon ah-EH-reh-oh
airport	*un aeroporto*
	oon ah-eh-roh-POR-toh
baggage	*i bagagli*
	ee bah-GAHL-yee
baggage check	*la consegna bagagli*
	lah kohn-SEHN-yah bah-GAHL-yee
boarding pass	*la carta d'imbarco*
	lah KAHR-tah dee eem-BAHR-koh

carry-on luggage	*i bagagli a mano* ee bah-GAHL-yee ah MAH-noh
checked luggage	*i bagagli da stiva* ee bah-GAHL-yee dah STEE-vah
cart	*un carello* oon kah-REHL-loh
check-in desk	*il banco di check-in* eel BAHN-koh dee check-in
departures	*partenze* pahr-TEHN-zeh
early	*in anticipo* een ahn-TEE-chee-poh
late	*in ritardo* een ree-TAHR-doh
passenger	*il passeggero* eel pahs-sehj-JEHR-oh
passport	*il passaporto* eel pahs-sah-POHR-toh
pilot	*il pilota* eel pee-LOH-tah
security check	*il controllo di sicurezza* eel kohn-TROHL-loh dee see-koo-REHTS-sah
shuttle	*lo shuttle* loh shuttle
steward/stewardess	*l'assistente di bordo* lahs-sees-TEHN-teh dee BOHR-doh
visa	*il visto* eel VEES-toh

-FACT

You will notice that English is often used for terms related to international travel. *La hostess* can be used to mean stewardess, *il duty free* is a duty-free shop, *economy* and *coach* are widely used to refer to travel class options, many Italians will check in at *il check-in,* and *un volo con stopover* is a flight with a stopover.

Ticket Information

airline	*la compagnia aerea*
	lah kohm-pahn-YEE-ah ah-EH-reh-ah
first class	*la prima classe*
	lah PREE-mah KLAHS-say
flight	*il volo*
	eel VOH-loh
gate	*l'uscita*
	loo-SHEE-tah
one-way ticket	*un biglietto solo andata*
	oon-beel-YEH-toh soh-loh ahn-DAH-tah
round-trip ticket	*un biglietto andata e ritorno*
	oon-beel-YEH-toh ahn-DAH-tah eh
	ree-TOHR-noh
terminal	*il terminal*
	eel terminal

Travel Verbs

to board	*imbarcare*
	eem-BAHR-kah-ray
to buy a ticket	*fare il biglietto*
	fah-ray eel beel-YEH-toh
to check bags	*consegnare i bagagli*
	kohn-sehn-YAH-ray ee bah-GAHL-yee
to make a	*fare una prenotazione*
reservation	fah-ray oo-nah preh-noh-tat-see-YOH-nay
to sit down	*sedersi* or *accomodarsi*
	seh-DEHR-see /ahk-koh-moh-DAHR-see
to take off	*decollare*
	deh-kohl-LAH-ray
to land	*atterrare*
	aht-teh-RAHR-ray

Baggage Claim, Immigration, and Customs

Before you can enjoy a nice dish of *pasta alla carbonara*, you have to get out of the airport. The following list of terms will help you get through customs smoothly.

Arrivals and Baggage

arrivals	*arrivi*
	ahr-REE-vee
baggage claim	*il ritiro bagagli*
	eel ree-TEE-roh bah-GAHL-yee
lost luggage	*i bagagli smarriti*
	ee bah-GAHL-yee smahr-REE-tee
My luggage is lost.	*I miei bagagli sono smarriti.*
	ee myay bah-GAHL-yee soh-noh
	smahr-REE-tee

Immigration and Customs

immigration	*l'immigrazione* lee-mee-grahts-ee-OH-nay
last name	*il cognome* eel kohn-YOH-may
first name	*il nome* eel noh-may
customs	*la dogana* lah doh-GAH-nah
nothing to declare	*niente da dichiarare* nee-EHN-tay dah deek-yah-RAH-ray
customs declaration form	*il modula dogana* eel MOH-doo-loh doh-GAH-nah

Here's my passport.
Ecco il mio passaporto.
ehk-koh eel mee-oh pahs-sah-POHR-toh

I have a visa.
Ho un visto.
oh oon VEES-toh

I don't have a visa.
Non ho un visto.
nohn oh oon VEES-toh

I would like to declare . . .
Vorrei dichiarare . . .
vohr-ray deek-yah-RAH-ray

Train Vocabulary

Traveling by train is often cheaper, faster, and more convenient than traveling by airplane or car within Italy, though there are some exceptions. Italy's bullet train, the Eurostar, offers fast, affordable, comfortable, and somewhat reliable service between major cities. Train travel from major cities to smaller cities and towns is certainly an affordable option, but it can add time to your trip, especially in southern Italy.

arrival	*arrivo*	ahr-REE-voh
cabin	*scompartimento*	skohm-pahr-tee-MEHN-toh
car	*carrozza*	kahr-ROH-tsah
chief conductor	*capotreno*	kah-poh-TREH-noh
conductor	*controllore*	kohn-trohl-LOH-reh
corridor	*corridoio*	kohr-ree-DOH-yoh
departure	*partenza*	pahr-TEHN-tzah
family offer	*offerta*	ohf-FEHR-tah
	famiglia	fah-MEE-lyah
first class	*prima classe*	PREE-mah KLAHS-seh
luggage rack	*retina* or	reh-TEE-nah/
(overhead)	*portabagagli*	pohr-tah-bah-GAH-lyee
nonsmokers	*non fumatori*	nohn foo-mah-TOH-ree
smokers	*fumatori*	foo-mah-TOH-ree
platform	*binario*	bee-NAH-ree-oh
railway	*ferrovia*	fehr-roh-VEE-ah
reservation	*prenotazione*	preh-noh-tah-TZYO-neh
restaurant car	*carrozza*	kahr-ROH-tzah
	ristorante	ree-stoh-RAHN-teh
seat	*posto*	POH-stoh
second class	*seconda*	seh-KOHN-dah
	classe	KLAHS-seh

sleeper car	*vagone*	vah-GOH-neh
	letto	LEHT-toh
sleeping compartment	*cuccetta*	koo-CHEHT-tah
station	*stazione*	stah-TZYOH-neh
supplement	*supplemento*	soop-pleh-MEHN-toh
ticket	*biglietto*	bee-LYEHT-toh
ticket office	*biglietteria*	bee-lyeht-tehr-REE-ah
toilet	*toilette*	twah-LEHT
tracks	*binari*	bee-NAH-ree
train	*treno*	TREH-noh
validate	*timbrare*	teem-BRAH-reh
window	*finestrino*	fee-neh-STREE-noh

The names of some Italian cities are spelled and pronounced differently in English. Here is a list of some of Italy's major cities, with their Italian spellings and pronunciations.

English	Italian	Pronunciation
Florence	*Firenze*	fee-REHN-tzeh
Leghorn	*Livorno*	lee-VOHR-noh
Mantua	*Mantova*	MAHN-toh-vah
Milan	*Milano*	mee-LAH-noh
Naples	*Napoli*	NAH-poh-lee
Rome	*Roma*	ROH-mah
Sienna	*Siena*	SYEH-nah
Turin	*Torino*	toh-REE-noh
Venice	*Venezia*	veh-NEH-tzyah

Some Useful Phrases for Train Travel

Sorry, is this the train to . . . ?	*Mi scusi, è questo il treno per . . . ?* mee SKOO-zee, eh KWEH-stoh eel TREH-noh pehr
Good morning, I have booked a seat . . .	*Buon giorno, ho prenotato il posto . . .* bwohn JOHR-noh, oh preh-noh-TAH-toh eel POH-sto
How long until we get to . . . ?	*Fra quanto si arriva a . . . ?* frah KWAHN-toh see ahr-REE-vah ah
Is the train late?	*Il treno è in ritardo?* eel TREH-noh eh een ree-TAHR-doh
Is this seat taken?	*È libero questo posto?* eh LEE-beh-roh KWEH-stoh POH-stoh
Yes, have a seat.	*Prego, si accomodi.* PREH-goh, see ahk-KOH-moh-dee
No, it's occupied.	*No, è occupato.* noh, eh ohk-koo-PAH-toh

At the Hotel

You're jet-lagged and in need of a nap, a shower, and a bite to eat. All you have is a few euros and this book. The following useful terms and expressions will help satisfy your every need.

I would like a room for/with . . .	*Vorrei una camera per/con . . .*
one night	*una notte* oo-nah NOHT-tay
two nights	*due notti* doo-eh NOHT-tee
one person	*una persona* oo-nah pehr-SOH-nah

two people	*due persone*
	doo-eh pehr-SOH-neh
two beds	*due letti*
	doo-eh LEHT-tee
a double bed	*un letto matrimoniale*
	oon LEHT-toh
	mah-tree-moh-nee-AH-lay
a shower in the room	*con bagno*
	kohn BAHN-yoh
a bathtub	*una vasca da bagno*
	oo-nah VAHS-kah dah BAHN-yoh
a toilet	*un toilette*
	oon twah-LEHT
a television	*un televisore*
	oon teh-leh-vee-ZOHR-ah
a telephone	*un telefono*
	oon teh-LEH-foh-noh
air conditioning	*il climatizzatore*
	eel klee-mah-teets-sah-TOHR-ay

Is there a(n) . . . ?	*Cè . . . ?* cheh
elevator	*un ascensore*
	oon ah-shehn-SOH-ray
hairdresser/barber	*un parucchiere/un barbiere*
	oon pah-rook-YEH-ray/oon bahrb-YEH-ray
parking lot	*un parcheggio*
	oon pahr-KEHJ-joh
restaurant	*un ristorante*
	oon rees-toh-RAHN-tay
pool	*una piscina*
	oo-nah pee-SHEE-nah

-SSENTIAL

There are many privately owned bed and break-fasts in Italy, commonly referred to as *pensioni*. Amenities tend to be on the slim side, but they often make up for it in character and person-ality. Be advised—the small *pensioni* often have a shared bathroom on each floor. Be sure to clarify when you're making a reservation that you would prefer a room *con bagno*.

Navigating Your Hotel

first floor (U.S.), ground floor (Italy)	*pian terreno*	pee-YAHN tehr-REH-noh
second floor (U.S.), first floor (Italy)	*primo piano*	PREE-moh pee-YAH-noh
hallway	*il corridoio*	eel kohr-ree-DOY-yoh
room	*la camera*	lah KAH-meh-rah
door	*la porta*	lah POHR-tah
window	*la finestra*	lah fee-NESS-trah
bed	*il letto*	eel LEHT-toh
pillow	*il cuscino*	eel koo-SHEE-noh
lamp	*la lampada*	lah LAHM-pah-dah
bathroom	*il bagno*	eel BAHN-yoh
towel	*l'asciugamano*	lah-shoo-gah-MAH-noh
wake-up call	*il servizio sveglia*	eel sehr-VEETS-see-oh SVEHL-yah

What time is check in/check out?
A che ora è il check in/il check out?
ah keh oh-rah eh eel check in/eel check out

Can I rent a car or a moped?
È possibile noleggiare un auto o un motorino?
eh pohs-SEE-bee-lay noh-lehj-JAH-ray oon ou-toh oh
    oon moh-toh-REE-noh

What kind of breakfast do you serve?
Che tipo di colazione servite?
keh tee-poh dee koh-lahts-see-YOH-neh sehr-VEE-teh

What time is breakfast served?
A che ora viene servita la colazione?
ah keh oh-rah VYEH-neh sehr-VEE-tah lah koh-lahts-
    see-YOH-neh

Does your hotel have an elevator? A garage?
Il vostro albergo dispone di un ascensore? Un garage?
eel VOHS-troh ahl-BEHR-goh dees-POH-neh dee oon
    ah-shehn-SOH-ray/oon garage

Is Internet access available for guests?
*Esiste una postazione Internet a disposizione degli
    ospiti dell'albergo?*
eh-ZEES-teh oo-nah poh-stahts-see-OH-ney Internet
    ah dee-spoh-zeets-YOH-nay dehl-yee OHS-pee-tee
    dehl ahl-BEHR-goh

How far away is the train station? (The airport?)
*Quanto dista la stazione centrale dei treni
(l'aeroporto) dal vostro albergo?*
kwahn-toh dees-tah lah staht-see-YOH-nay chehn-
TRAH-lay day treh-nee (leh-roh-POHR-toh) dahl
vohs-troh ahl-BEHR-goh

How do we get to your hotel from the airport?
*Come possiamo raggiungere il vostro albergo
dall'aeroporto?*
koh-meh pohs-see-YAH-moh rah-JOON-jeh-ray eel
vohs-troh ahl-BEHR-goh dahl ah-eh-roh-POHR-toh

How far is the closest bus stop?
Quanto dista la fermata più vicina dell'autobus?
kwahn-toh dees-tah lah fehr-MAH-tah pyou vee-
CHEE-nah dehl OW-toh-boos

Can I reserve museum tickets through the hotel?
*È possibile prenotare i biglietti dei musei direttamente
dal vostro albergo?*
eh pohs-SEE-bee-lay preh-noh-TAH-ray ee beel-YEH-
tee day mooz-eh-ee dee-reht-tah-MEHN-tay dahl
vohs-troh ahl-BEHR-goh

Is the hotel in the historical center of the city?
L'albergo è situato nel centro storico?
lahl-BEHR-goh eh see-too-AH-toh nehl chehn-troh
STOH-ree-koh

Settling Your Bill

Sadly, your trip is coming to an end. Here are some useful expressions to help get your hotel bill settled.

How much is it?
Quanto è?
KWAHN-toh eh

I would like to pay my bill.
Vorrei saldare il conto.
vohr-ray sahl-DAH-ray eel kohn-toh

I would like to pay . . .	*Vorrei pagare . . .* (vohr-ray pah-GAH-ray)
in cash	*con contanti*
	kohn kohn-TAHN-tee
with traveler's checks	*con i travelers checks*
	kohn ee travelers checks
with a credit card	*con la carta di credito*
	kohn lah kahr-ta dee KREH-dee-toh

-ALERT

Be sure to ask ahead of time if the hotel takes credit cards or traveler's checks. Small, family-run hotels and *pensioni* might only accept cash.

Chapter 6

Getting Around Town

Asking directions, hailing a cab, and reading a bus schedule are all things you might want to know how to do for your upcoming trip. This chapter will help you find your way around.

Asking for Directions

Perhaps the most frequently asked questions in all tourist destinations have to do with asking for directions. Here are some useful phrases to ask for help finding your way around:

Excuse me, where is . . . ?
Mi scusi, dov'è . . . ?
mee skoo-zee doh-veh

Is it very far?
È molto lontano?
eh mohl-toh lohn-TAH-noh

How long will it take by car?
Quanto ci vorrà in macchina?
kwahn-toh chee vohr-RAH een mahk-KEE-nah

How far away is the station?
Quanto dista la stazione?
kwahn-toh dees-tah lah staht-see-OH-nay

How much further to . . . ?
Quanto manca a . . . ?
kwahn-toh mahn-kah ah

Excuse me, I'm lost.
Scusi, mi sono perso.
skoo-zee mee soh-noh pehr-soh

Where is the nearest gas station?
Dove si trova il distributore di benzina più vicino?
doh-veh see troh-vah eel dees-tree-boo-TOH-ray dee
    ben-TSEE-nah pyou vee-CHEE-noh

It's close by.
È a due passi.
eh ah doo-ay pahs-see

Can you tell me where it is?
Può dirmi dov'è?
poo-owe deer-mee dohv-EH

Can you give me directions to . . . ?
Può indicarmi la strada per . . . ?
poo-owe een-dee-KAHR-mee lah strah-dah pehr

Directions

Go straight.	*Vai diritto.*	veye dee-REET-toh
Turn left.	*Gira a sinistra.*	jee-rah ah see-NEES-trah
Turn right.	*Gira a destra.*	jee-rah a dess-trah
to the left	*alla sinistra*	ahl-lah see-NEES-trah
to the right	*alla destra*	ahl-lah dess-trah
straight ahead	*sempre diritto*	sehm-preh dee-REET-toh
next to	*accanto a*	ahk-KAHN-toh ah
in front of	*davanti a*	dah-vahn-tee ah
in back of	*dietro*	dee-EH-troh
near (to)	*vicino a*	vee-CHEE-noh ah
far (from)	*lontano da*	lohn-TAH-noh dah
north	*nord*	nohrd
south	*sud*	sood
east	*est*	ehst
west	*ovest*	oh-vehst

Some Useful Destinations

You've left your map back in the hotel room, and you know the museum you want to visit is around here somewhere. Now if you could only remember the word for museum! This section presents some useful place names found in most cities.

bank	*banca*	bahn-kah
bus stop	*la fermata*	lah fehr-MAH-tah
	dell'autobus	dehll AHW-toh-boos
cathedral	*cattedrale*	kaht-teh-DRAH-lay
church	*chiesa*	kee-AY-zah
coffee shop	*bar*	bahr
fountain	*fontana*	fohn-TAH-nah
gardens	*giardini*	jahr-DEE-nee
hotel	*hotel/albergo*	oh-tell/ahl-BEHR-goh
monument	*monumento*	mohn-oo-MEHN-toh
museum	*museo*	moo-ZAY-oh
open-air market	*mercato*	mehr-KAH-toh
park	*parco*	pahr-koh
restaurant	*ristorante*	rees-toh-RAHN-tay
supermarket	*supermercato*	soo-pehr-mehr-KAH-toh
theater	*teatro*	tay-AH-troh

Types of Transportation

Many Italian cities offer a full range of transportation options. Rome, Milan, Palermo, and Naples all have subway systems that are reasonably safe and reliable.

bicycle	*la bicicletta*	lah bee-chee-KLEH-tah
bus	*l'autobus*	LAHW-toh-boos
bus stop	*la fermata*	lah fehr-MAH-tah
	dell'autobus	dehll AHW-toh-boos
car	*la macchina*	lah MAH-kee-nah
moped	*il motorino*	eel moh-toh-REE-noh
motorcycle	*la moto*	lah moh-toh
subway	*la metropolitana*	lah meh-troh-poh-lee-TAH-nah
taxi	*il taxi*	eel tahk-see
taxi stand	*la stazione*	lah staht-see-OH-nay
	dei taxi	day tahk-see
train	*il treno*	eel tray-noh
train station	*la stazione*	lah staht-see-OH-nay

-SSENTIAL

> Water taxis (*motoscafi*) and water busses (*vaporetti*) are available in Venice. Taxis in Venice can be expensive, but the *vaporetti* are very reasonable and reliable—and they're fun, too!

Renting a Car

Public transportation and taxis are readily available in all Italian cities, but you may want to rent a car to explore off the beaten path. Keep in mind that standard transmissions in cars are the norm in Italy. If you need a car with an automatic transmission, it is best to make a reservation before you leave for your trip.

I'd like to rent a car.
Vorrei noleggiare una macchina.
vohr-ray noh-lehj-JAH-ray oo-nah MAH-kee-nah

economy car	*macchina piccola* MAH-kee-nah PEEK-koh-lah
midsize car	*macchina media* MAH-kee-nah MEH-dee-ah
full-size car	*macchina grande* MAH-kee-nah grahn-day
convertible	*decapotabile* deh-kah-poh-TAH-bee-leh
truck	*camion* KAH-mee-ohn
automatic	*automatico* ahw-toh-MAH-tee-koh

-ALERT

Italian law requires that non–European Union citizens possess an International Driving Permit (IDP). Car rental agencies are increasingly checking for the IDP when you pick up your rental car. You will need both the IDP and your current driver's license when traveling. You can apply for an IDP at your local American Automobile Association (AAA) or American Automobile Touring Alliance.

How much will it cost?
Quanto costa?
kwahn-toh kohs-tah

I'd like to pay by credit card.
Vorrei pagare con la carta di credito.
vohr-ray pah-GAH-ray kohn lah kahr-tah dee KREH-dee-toh

Finding Your Way Around

This section presents some useful words and phrases to help you navigate the open road.

Street Smarts

accident	*un incidente*
	oon een-chee-DEHN-tay
all routes/	*tutte le direzioni*
directions	toot-teh leh dee-rehts-YOH-nee
bypass road	*un tangenziale*
	oon tahn-jehnts-YAH-lay
dead end	*strada senza uscita*
	strah-dah sehn-tsah oo-SHEE-tah
diesel	*il diesel*
	eel dee-zehl
driver	*l'autista*
	lahw-TEES-tah
gas	*la benzina*
	lah behn-TSEE-nah
gas station	*un distributore di benzina*
	oon dees-tree-boo-TOH-ray dee ben-TSEE-nah

highway	*un'autostrada*
	oon-AHW-toh-strah-dah
lane	*una corsia*
	oo-nah kohr-SEE-ah
lights	*i fari*
	ee fah-ree
no parking	*vietato parcheggiare*
	vee-eh-TAH-toh pahr-kehj-JAH-ray
no stopping	*vietata la sosta*
	vee-eh-TAH-tah lah sohs-tah
one way	*senso unico*
	sehn-soh OO-nee-koh
pedestrian	*il pedonale*
	eel peh-doh-NAH-lay
pedestrian	*le strisce pedonali*
crosswalk	le stree-sheh peh-doh-NAH-lee
rush hour	*l'ora di punta*
	loh-rah dee poon-tah
speed limit	*il limite di velocità*
	eel LEE-mee-teh dee veh-loh-chee-TAH
stop	*stop*
	stohp
traffic lights	*il semaforo*
	eel seh-MAH-foh-roh

Car Talk

car	*una macchina/un' automobile/un'auto*
	oo-nah MAH-kee-nah/oon ahw-toh-MOH-bee-leh/oon ahw-toh
car hood	*il cofano*
	eel KOH-fah-noh
radio	*la radio*
	lah RAH-dee-oh

rearview mirror	*lo specchietto*
	loh spehk-KYEH-toh
seatbelt	*la cintura di sicurezza*
	lah cheen-TOO-rah dee see-koo-REHTS-sah
steering wheel	*il volante*
	eel voh-LAHN-tay
tire	*la gomma/il pneumatico*
	lah gohm-mah/eel neh-oo-MAH-tee-koh
trunk	*il bagagliaio*
	eel bah-GAHL-yeye-oh
	(pronounced like the English "eye")
windshield	*la parabrezza*
	lah pah-rah-BREHTS-sah
windshield	*i tergicristalli*
wipers	ee tehr-jee-krees-TAHL-lee

Useful Driving Verbs

Here are some essential verbs related to driving:

to pass/overtake	*sorpassare*
	sohr-pahs-SAH-ray
to slow down	*rallentare*
	rahl-lehn-TAH-ray
to yield	*dare la precedenza*
	dah-ray lah preh-cheh-DEHN-tsah
to get a ticket	*prendere una multa*
	PREHN-deh-ray oo-nah mool-tah
to give a ticket	*dare una multa*
	dah-ray oo-nah mool-tah
to pull over to the	*accostare*
side of the road	ahk-kohs-TAH-ray

to get gas	*fare la benzina*
	fah-ray lah ben-TSEE-nah
to fill it up	*fare il pieno*
	fah-ray eel pyeh-noh
to hitchhike	*fare l'autostop*
	fah-ray LAHW-toh-stohp
to park	*parcheggiare*
	pahr-kehj-JAH-ray
to turn	*girare*
	jee-RAH-ray
to drive	*guidare*
	gwee-DAH-ray
to travel	*viaggiare*
	vee-ahj-JAH-ray
to cross	*attraversare*
	aht-trah-vehr-SAH-ray
to go	*andare*
	ahn-DAH-ray
to buckle your seat belt	*allacciare la cintura di sicurezza*
	ahl-lahch-CHAH-ray lah cheen-TOO-rah
	dee see-koo-REHTS-sah

-SSENTIAL

Italy has a reputation for chaotic streets and highways. Though your initial attempt at driving in Italy may be intimidating at first, you will find Italian drivers to be aggressive but entirely competent. Italian traffic is often described as "organized chaos," which to some extent is true.

Chapter 7

The Art of Dining Out

Italy is known for its world-class cuisine. Culinary traditions and styles vary from region to region (and from city to city as well). Knowing how to order your meal will only enhance your dining experience.

Dining Out

Here are some general phrases related to dining in a restaurant:

Meals and Courses

meal	*il pasto*	eel pahs-toh
breakfast	*la colazione*	lah koh-lahts-YOH-neh
lunch	*il pranzo*	eel prahn-zoh
dinner	*la cena*	lah cheh-nah
snack	*la merendina*	lah meh-rehn-DEE-nah
antipasto	*gli antipasti*	lyee ahn-tee-PAHS-tee
first course	*il primo (piatto)*	eel pree-moh
soup	*la zuppa,*	lah dsoop-ah,
	la minestra,	lah mee-NESS-trah,
	la minestrone	lah mee-ness-TROH-neh
second course	*il secondo (piatto)*	eel seh-KOHN-doh
vegetable course	*il contorno*	eel kohn-TOHR-noh
salad	*l'insalata*	leen-sah-LAH-tah
dessert	*il dessert/il dolce*	eel deh-sehrt,
		eel dohl-chay

At the Restaurant

restaurant	*il ristorante*	eel rees-toh-RAHN-tay
(small) restaurant	*la trattoria*	lah trah-toh-REE-ah
public house/inn	*l'osteria*	lohs-teh-REE-ah
buffet-style	*la tavola*	lah TAH-voh-lah
restaurant	*calda*	kahl-dah
pizzeria	*la pizzeria*	lah peet-seh-REE-ah
kitchen or cuisine	*la cucina*	lah koo-CHEE-nah
dining room	*la sala*	lah sah-lah
waiter	*il cameriere*	eel kah-meh-RYEH-ray
waitress	*la cameriera*	lah kah-meh-RYEH-rah

cook	*il cuoco/*	eel kwoh-koh/
	lo chef	loh shehf
pizza maker	*il pizzaiolo*	eel peet-seye-OH-loh
bartender	*il barista*	eel bah-REES-tah

-SSENTIAL

A full Italian meal consists of *antipasto, primo* (usually a pasta or rice dish), *secondo* (meat, poultry, or fish) with *contorni* (vegetables), *insalata* (dressed with oil, vinegar, and salt), and *il dolce* (dessert).

What to Order?

Ah, so many choices, and so few days to try them all. It's easy to find a restaurant in a touristy area that offers Italian-American food (spaghetti with alfredo sauce, spaghetti and meatballs, and so on). Try to find something that's off the beaten path, and certainly try to order something that you've never tried before—you'll almost always be pleasantly surprised!

Antipasto

From city to city and region to region, you will find thousands of different types of *antipasti*. Many restaurants will have a buffet table set up with numerous types of antipasti to choose from. The following are some of the more common items you can find throughout Italy.

Antipasto

le acciughe leh ah-CHOO-geh	anchovies
l'affettato misto lahf-feht-TAH-toh mees-toh	various cold cuts
l'arancino lah-rahn-CHEE-noh	rice ball filled with meat and cheese
la bruschetta lah broo-SKEH-tah	toasted bread topped with diced tomatoes
la bruschetta col salmone broo-SKEH-tah kohn sahl-MOH-neh	toasted bread topped with salmon
i calamari fritti ee kah-lah-MAH-ree free-tee	fried squid
la caponata siciliana lah kah-poh-NAH-tah see-cheel-YAH-nah	eggplant and tomato stew
il caprese eel kah-PRAY-zay	mozzarella, tomatoes, fresh basil, and olive oil
i carciofi ee kahr-CHOH-fee	artichokes
il carpaccio eel kahr-PAH-choh	raw beef very thinly sliced
la focaccia lah foh-KAH-chah	flat bread
frutti di mare froo-tee dee mah-ray	mixed seafood
i funghi imbottiti ee foon-gee eem-boh-TEE-tee	stuffed mushrooms
la giardiniera lah jahr-deen-YEH-rah	pickled vegetables
gli involtini di prosciutto lyee een-vohl-TEE-nee dee pro-SHOO-toh	rolled, stuffed prosciutto

le lumache leh loo-MAH-keh	snails
la peperonata lah peh-peh-roh-NAH-tah	peppers sautéed with oil and capers
i pomodori farciti di tonno ee poh-moh-DOH-ree fahr-CHEE-tee dee tohn-noh	tomatoes stuffed with tuna
i pomodori ripieni con riso ee poh-moh-DOH-ree ree-PYEH-nee kohn ree-zoh	tomatoes stuffed with rice
le olive condite oh-LEE-veh kohn-DEE-teh	marinated olives
il patè di vitello pah-TEH dee vee-TEHL-loh	veal patè
prosciutto e melone proh-SHOO-toh eh meh-LOH-neh	prosciutto and melon
le seppioline alla griglia sehp-pyoh-LEE-neh ahl-lah greel-yah	grilled cuttlefish
sauté di vongole sohw-teh dee VOHN-goh-leh	sautéed clams
i gamberi ee GAHM-beh-ree	shrimp
vongole in graticola VOHN-goh-leh een grah-TEE-koh-lah	clams with parsley and bread crumbs
vongole inciocchite VOHN-goh-leh een-chohk-KEE-teh	steamed clams

First Course Dishes: *I primi piatti*

The first course mainly consists of either a pasta or rice dish. There are dozens of different types of pastas, some of which are unique to certain areas in Italy. Each type of pasta is usually matched with a specific sauce based on various factors. For example, thin, delicate pastas like angel hair or thin spaghetti, are better served with light, thin sauces; thicker pasta shapes like fettuccine work well with heavier sauces, and pasta shapes with holes or ridges are perfect for chunkier sauces. You may find that some Italians will substitute a pizza for the first course.

I tipi di pasta (Types of Pasta)

agnolotti ahn-yoh-LOHT-tee	similar to ravioli but smaller; this is usually stuffed with meat, cheese, or vegetables
cannelloni kahn-nehl-LOH-nee	large, tube-shaped pasta, usually filled with meat or cheese
cappellini kahp-pehl-LEE-nee	very thin pasta, often called angel hair
conchiglie kohn-KEE-lyeh	shells of pasta
farfalle fahr-FAHL-leh	shaped like a butterfly or bow tie
fettuccine feht-too-CHEE-neh	thin noodles that are somewhat wider than spaghetti
fusilli foo-ZEE-lee	corkscrews
gemelli jeh-MEHL-lee	single S-shaped strands of pasta twisted in a loose spiral
gnocchi nyohk-kee	potato or ricotta-based pasta dumplings
lasagne lah-ZAHN-yeh	broad, flat noodles, usually baked with meat, cheese, and tomato sauce
linguine leen-GWEE-neh	flat noodles, wider than spaghetti, but narrower than fettuccine

maltagliati mahl-tahl-YAH-tee	flat, roughly cut triangles
orecchiette oh-rehk-KYEH-teh	small bowl-shaped pasta
pappardelle pahp-pahr-DEHL-leh	broad, long noodles
penne pehn-neh	short pasta tubes
ravioli rah-vee-OH-lee	pillows of pasta, stuffed with cheese, meat, or vegetables
rigatoni ree-gah-TOH-nee	short, large tubes
rotelle roh-TEHL-leh	wagon wheel-shaped pasta
rotini roh-TEE-nee	double-edged spiral, tightly wound
spaghetti spah-GEHT-tee	long, thin strands of pasta
tagliatelle tahl-yah-TEHL-leh	long, flat strands of pasta
tortellini tohr-tehl-LEE-nee	small, folded pillows of pasta, usually stuffed with cheese, meat, or vegetables

Types of Pasta Sauces

boscaiola bohs-keye-OH-lah	tomatoes, butter, cheese, mushrooms, olive oil, garlic
bolognese boh-lohn-YEH-zeh	meat, tomatoes, cheese
carbonara kahr-boh-NAH-rah	olive oil, cheese, egg, bacon
diavolo DYAH-voh-loh	tomato sauce with hot spices

genovese jeh-noh-VEH-seh	basil, pine nuts, garlic, olive oil
marinara mah-ree-NAH-rah	tomatoes, olive oil, garlic, sometimes olives
napoletana nah-poh-leh-TAH-nah	cheese, tomatoes, herbs
puttanesca poot-tah-NESS-kah	tomatoes, black olives, peppers, olive oil, garlic
quattro formaggi kwaht-troh fohr-MAH-jee	literally, four cheeses
siciliana see-cheel-YAH-nah	provolone cheese and eggplant

-FACT

The word *peperone* in Italian means pepper, as in
the vegetable. A pepperoni pizza in Italian is *una
pizza con salamino piccante*.

Pizza

asparagi ahs-PAH-rah-jee	tomato sauce, mozzarella, asparagus
bismark beez-mahrk	tomato sauce, mozzarella, egg
bufala BOO-fah-lah	tomato sauce, buffalo mozzarella
capricciosa kahp-pree-CHOH-zah	tomato sauce, mozzarella, prosciutto, mushrooms, egg, artichokes, sausage, olives
carciofini kahr-choh-FEE-nee	tomato sauce, mozzarella, artichokes

diavola DYAH-voh-lah	tomato sauce, mozzarella, anchovies, black olives, capers, spicy salami
funghi foon-gee	tomato sauce, mozzarella, mushrooms
funghi porcini foon-gee pohr-CHEE-nee	tomato sauce, mozzarella, porcini mushrooms
gorgonzola gohr-gohn-ZOH-lah	tomato sauce, mozzarella, gorgonzola
marinara mah-ree-NAH-rah	tomato sauce, garlic, oregano
margherita mahr-geh-REE-tah	tomato sauce, mozzarella
melanzane meh-lahn-ZAH-neh	tomato sauce, mozzarella, eggplant
napoli NAH-poh-lee	tomato sauce, mozzarella, anchovies, capers, oregano
peperoni peh-peh-ROH-nee	tomato sauce, mozzarella, peppers
primavera pree-mah-VEH-rah	mozzarella, sliced tomato
prosciutto cotto proh-SHOO-toh koht-toh	tomato sauce, mozzarella, cured ham
prosciutto crudo proh-SHOO-toh kroo-doh	tomato sauce, mozzarella, cooked ham
pugliese pool-YEH-zay	tomato sauce, mozzarella, anchovies, olives, onion, oregano
quattro formaggi kwaht-troh fohr-MAH-jee	tomato sauce, mozzarella, fontina, gorgonzola, pecorino cheeses
quattro stagioni kwaht-troh stah-JOH-nee	tomato sauce, mozzarella, prosciutto, mushrooms, egg, artichokes, olives

romana roh-mah-nah	tomato sauce, mozzarella, anchovies, capers, oregano, olives
salame piccante sah-LAH-meh peek-KAHN-teh	tomato sauce, mozzarella, spicy salami
salsiccia sahl-SEE-chah	tomato sauce, mozzarella, sausage
tonno tohn-noh	tomato sauce, mozzarella, tuna
verdure vehr-DOO-reh	tomato sauce, mozzarella, with assorted vegetables

Second Course Dishes: Meat, Fish, Poultry

beef	*il manzo*	eel man-zoh
chicken	*il pollo*	eel pohl-loh
ham	*il prosciutto*	eel proh-SHOOT-toh
hare	*il lepre*	eel leh-pray
lamb	*l'agnello*	lahn-YEHL-loh
liver	*il fegato*	eel FEH-gah-toh
meat	*la carne*	lah kahr-nay
pork	*il maiale*	eel meye-AH-lay
rabbit	*il coniglio*	eel koh-NEEL-yoh
sausage	*la salsiccia*	lah sahl-SEE-chah
seafood	*i frutti di mare*	ee froot-tee dee mah-ray
steak	*la bistecca*	lah bees-TEHK-kah
turkey	*il tacchino*	eel tahk-KEE-noh
veal	*il vitello*	eel vee-TEHL-loh

Meat Preparation

rare	*al sangue*	ahl sahn-gway
well done	*ben cotto*	behn-koht-toh

-SSENTIAL

Italians don't really have a term for "medium" cooked meat. The default is usually medium, but if you want it rare (*al sangue*), or well done (*ben cotto*), you'll have to ask for it specifically.

Dairy (*i latticini*)

butter	*il burro*	eel boo-roh
cheese	*il formaggio*	eel fohr-MAHJ-joh
milk	*il latte*	eel laht-tay
yogurt	*il yogurt*	eel yoh-gurt

Fruit (*le frutte*)

apple	*una mela*	oo-nah meh-lah
apricot	*un albicocca*	oon ahl-bee-KOHK-kah
banana	*una banana*	oo-nah bah-NAH-nah
blackberry	*una mora*	oo-nah moh-rah
blueberry	*un mirtillo*	oon meer-TEEL-loh
cherry	*una ciliegia*	oo-nah chee-LYEH-jah
grape	*un'uva*	oon-oo-vah
grapefruit	*un pompelmo*	oon pohm-PEHL-moh
lemon	*un limone*	oon lee-MOH-nay
orange	*un'arancia*	oon-ah-RAHN-chah
peach	*una pesca*	oo-nah pess-kah
pear	*una pera*	oo-nah peh-rah
raspberry	*un lampone*	oon lahm-POH-nay
strawberry	*una fragola*	oo-nah FRAH-goh-lah

Vegetables (*i legumi*)

artichoke	*il carcioffo*	eel kahr-CHOHF-foh
asparagus	*gli asparagi*	lyee ahs-PAH-rah-jee
beans	*i fagioli*	ee fah-JOH-lee
carrot	*la carotta*	la kah-ROHT-tah
cabbage	*il cavolo*	eel KAH-voh-loh
celery	*il sedano*	eel SEH-dah-noh
eggplant	*la melanzana*	lah meh-lahn-ZAH-nah
garlic	*l'aglio*	lahl-yoh
lettuce	*la lettuga*	lah leht-TOO-gah
onion	*la cipolla*	lah chee-POHL-lah
peas	*i piselli*	ee pee-ZEHL-lee
radish	*il ravanello*	eel rah-vah-NEHL-loh
spinach	*gli spinaci*	lyee spee-NAH-chee

Dessert (*i dolci*)

cake	*la torta*	lah tohr-tah
cookie	*il biscotto*	eel bees-KOHT-toh
fruit salad	*la macedonia*	lah mah-cheh-DOH-nee-ah
	di frutta	dee froot-tah
ice cream	*il gelato*	eel jeh-LAH-toh

Beverages: *Da bere*

Italy is one of the world's largest wine producers. You may be overwhelmed by the selection available in some restaurants. If you're not sure what to order, ask your waiter.

Beverages

after-dinner drink	*il digestivo*	eel dee-jess-TEE-voh
aperitif	*l'aperitivo*	lah-peh-reh-TEE-voh

beer	*la birra*	lah bee-rah
coffee	*il caffè*	eel kahf-FEH
red wine	*il vino rosso*	eel vee-noh rohs-soh
white wine	*il vino bianco*	eel vee-noh byahn-koh
wine	*il vino*	eel vee-noh
water	*l'acqua*	lahk-wah
	(minerale)	(mee-neh-RAH-leh)

-FACT

> When taking your order, the waiter may ask you,
> *E da bere?*, which translates as "Something to
> drink?" To ask for a wine recommendation, you
> might ask, *Può consigliarmi un buon vino?*

Dishes and Silverware

If you need to ask for another fork or napkin, here's the
vocabulary you'll need:

bowl	*la ciotola*	lah CHOH-toh-lah
cup	*la tazza*	lah taht-sah
fork	*la forchetta*	lah fohr-KEHT-tah
glass	*il bicchiere*	eel beek-KYEH-ray
knife	*il coltello*	eel kohl-TELL-loh
napkin	*il tovagliolo*	eel toh-vahl-YOH-loh
plate	*il piatto*	eel pyaht-toh
silverware	*le posate*	leh poh-ZAH-teh
spoon	*il cucchiaio*	eel kook-KYAH-yoh

Ordering Your Meal

Here are some useful words to help you order your meal:

to be hungry	*aver fame*	ah-VEHR fah-may
to be thirsty	*avere sete*	ah-veh-ray seh-teh
to order	*ordinare*	ohr-dee-NAH-ray
to drink	*bere*	beh-ray
to eat	*mangiare*	mahn-JAH-ray
check/bill	*il conto*	eel kohn-toh
cover charge	*il coperto*	eel koh-PEHR-toh
service charge	*il servizio*	eel sehr-VEETS-ee-oo
menu	*il menu*	eel meh-noo
tip	*la mancia*	lah mahn-chah
What would you like?	*Che cosa mangia?*	keh koh-zah mahn-jah
I would like . . .	*Io vorrei . . .*	ee-oo vohr-ray
I am a vegetarian.	*Sono vegetariano.*	soh-noh veh-jeh-tah-ree-AH-noh
I am on a diet.	*Sono a dieta.*	soh-noh ah dee-EH-tah
I am allergic.	*Sono allergico.*	soh-noh ahl-LEHR-jee-koh

-SSENTIAL

Some restaurants will add a cover charge—*il coperto*—and a service charge—*il servizio*—to your bill. This, by law, must be clearly marked on the menu. As a general rule, Italian waiters will not expect a tip, though adding a few euros to your payment will be appreciated.

Chapter 8
Shopping and Services

With credit card in hand, you're off to spend, spend, spend! From clothing to jewelry to artisanal products, this chapter will introduce you to the places you can spend money and the questions you should ask about your purchases.

Stores and Businesses

There are many places that will gladly accept your money in exchange for goods and services. Here is a list of the ones you might be most interested in:

bakery	*il fornaio*	eel fohr-NEYE-oh
butcher shop	*la macelleria*	lah mah-chehl-leh-REE-ah
delicatessen	*la salumeria*	lah sah-loo-meh-REE-ah
department store	*un grande magazzino*	oon grahn-day mah-gaht-SEE-noh
dry cleaner	*la lavanderia a secco*	lah lah-vahn-deh-REE-ah ah sehk-koh
fish market	*la pescheria*	lah pess-keh-REE-ah
fruit stand	*il fruttivendolo*	lah froo-tee-VEHN-doh-lah
grocery store	*alimentari*	ah-lee-mehn-TAH-ree
ice cream shop	*la gelateria*	lah jeh-lah-teh-REE-ah
jewelry shop	*la gioielleria*	lah joy-ehl-leh-REE-ah
newsstand	*l'edicola*	leh-DEE-koh-lah
outdoor market	*il mercato*	eel mehr-KAH-toh
pastry shop	*la pasticceria*	lah pahs-tee-cheh-REE-ah
pharmacy	*la farmacia*	lah far-mah-CHEE-ah
store	*il negozio*	eel neh-GOHT-see-oh
supermarket	*il supermercato*	eel soo-pehr-mehr-KAH-toh
tobacco shop	*il tabaccaio*	eel tah-bahk-KEYE-oh

-FACT

You will find that any deli shop, or *salumeria* in Italian, is likely to offer an extensive variety of local cured meats. Buy a loaf of bread, a jug of wine, and some cured meats for a delicious picnic meal.

Laundromat and Dry Cleaner

Did you spill some Chianti on the only dress shirt you brought with you? Perhaps a smattering of marinara sauce on your blouse? Laundromats and dry cleaners are there to help.

to wash	*lavare*	lah-VAH-ray
to dry clean	*lavare a secco*	lah-VAH-ray ah sehk-koh
to dry	*asciugare*	ah-shoo-GAH-ray
bleach	*la candeggina*	lah kahn-dehj-JEE-nah
dryer	*l'asciugatrice*	lah-shoo-gah-TREE-cheh
fabric softener	*l'ammorbidente*	lahm-mohr-bee-DEHN-teh
to do the laundry	*fare il bucato*	fah-ray eel boo-KAH-toh
soap	*il sapone*	eel sah-POH-nay
stain	*la macchia*	lah mahk-kyah
starch(ed)	*inamidato*	een-ah-mee-DAH-toh
washing machine	*la lavatrice*	lah lah-vah-TREE-cheh

Hair Salon and Barbershop

Italian hairstylists and barbers have the reputation of being among the best in the world. You'll find that prices can be reasonable, especially in a barber shop. Hey, you're on vacation—give it a try!

barber	*il barbiere*	eel bahr-BYEH-ray
beard	*la barba*	lah bahr-bah
beauty parlor	*la parrucheria*	lah pahr-rook-eh-REE-ah
brush	*la spazzola*	lah SPAHT-soh-lah
comb	*il pettine*	eel peht-tee-neh
curls	*i riccioli*	ee REE-choh-lee
dandruff	*la forfora*	lah FOHR-foh-rah

dry hair	*i capelli secchi*	ee kah-PEHL-lee sehk-kee
hair	*i capelli*	ee kah-PEHL-lee
haircut	*il taglio di capelli*	eel tahl-yoh dee kah-PEHL-lee
hairstyle	*la pettinatura*	lah peh-tee-nah-TOO-rah
hairstylist	*il parruchiere*	eel pahr-rook-YEH-ray
long	*lungo*	loon-goh
moustache	*i baffi*	ee bahf-fee
oily hair	*i capelli grassi*	ee kah-PEHL-lee grah-see
part	*la riga*	lah ree-gah
scalp massage	*la frizione*	lah freets-YOH-neh
short	*corto*	kohr-toh
strand	*la frangetta*	lah frahn-JEHT-tah
trim	*una spuntatina*	oo-nah spoon-tah-TEE-nah
wig	*la parrucca*	lah pahr-ROOK-kah
wisp	*la ciocca di capelli*	lah chohk-kah dee kah-PEHL-lee

Verbs

to blow dry	*asciugare con il phon*
	ah-shoo-GAH-ray kohn eel fohn
to curl	*arricciare i capelli*
	ah-reech-CHAH-ray ee kah-PEHL-lee
to cut	*tagliare*
	tahl-YAH-ray
to perm	*fare la permanente*
	fah-ray lah pehr-mah-NEHN-tay
to shave	*fare la barba/radere*
	fah-ray lah bahr-bah/RAH-deh-ray
to wash	*lavare*
	lah-vah-ray

to tease	*cotonare*	koh-toh-NAH-ray
to do someone's hair	*fare i capelli*	fah-ray ee kah-PEHL-lee
to dye/to color	*tingere*	TEEN-jeh-ray
to brush	*spazzolare*	spahts-soh-LAH-ray
to comb	*pettinare*	peht-tee-NAH-ray

Clothing and Jewelry

Milan and Rome are at the center of the world's fashion and jewelry industries. Besides the larger department stores and big-name shops, you will find numerous boutique shops that offer stylish (and affordable!) clothing. Shopping can be fun, but it can be overwhelming, too, so be sure to pace yourself.

Clothing

bathing suit	*il costume da bagno*	eel kohs-TOO-meh dah bahn-yoh
belt	*la cintura*	lah cheen-TOO-rah
blouse	*la camicetta*	lah kah-mee-CHEHT-tah
boots	*gli stivali*	lyee stee-VAH-lee
bra	*il reggiseno*	eel reh-jee-SEH-noh
button	*il bottone*	eel boht-TOH-neh
cloth, fabric, material	*il tessuto*	eel tehs-SOO-toh
clothes	*i vestiti*	ee vehs-TEE-tee

color	*il colore*	eel koh-LOH-ray
cotton	*il cotone*	eel koh-TOH-nay
dress	*il vestito*	eel vehs-TEE-toh
	donna	doh-nah
footwear	*la calzatura*	lah kahl-tsah-TOO-rah
glasses	*gli occhiali*	lyee ohk-KYAH-lee
gloves	*i guanti*	ee gwahn-tee
handbag	*la borsa*	lah bohr-sah
hat	*il cappello*	eel kahp-PEHL-loh
jacket	*la giacca*	lah jahk-kah
jeans	*i jeans*	ee jeans
leather	*il cuoio*	eel kwoy-oh
lining	*la fodera*	lah FOH-deh-rah
lipstick	*il rossetto*	eel rohs-SEHT-toh
makeup	*il trucco*	eel trook-koh
overcoat	*il cappotto*	eel kahp-POHT-toh
pajamas	*il pigiama*	eel pee-JAH-mah
panties	*le mutandine*	leh moo-tahn-DEE-neh
pants	*i pantaloni*	ee pahn-toh-LOH-nee
perfume	*il profumo*	eel proh-FOO-moh
pocket	*la tasca*	lah tahs-kah
raincoat	*l'impermeabile*	leem-pehr-mee-AH-bee-leh
sandals	*i sandali*	ee SAHN-dah-lee
scarf	*la sciarpa*	lah shahr-pah
shirt	*la camicia*	lah kah-MEE-chah
shoelace	*il laccio*	eel lahch-choh
shoes	*le scarpe*	leh skahr-peh
silk	*la seta*	lah seh-tah
skirt	*la gonna*	lah gohn-nah
sleeve	*la manica*	lah MAH-nee-kah
slippers	*le pantofole*	leh pahn-TOH-foh-leh

sneakers	*le scarpe da ginnastica*	leh skahr-peh dah jeen-NAHS-tee-kah
socks	*il calzini*	eel kahl-TSEE-nee
spike heel	*il tacco a spillo*	eel tahk-koh ah speel-loh
stocking	*la calza*	lah kahl-tsah
suit	*il completo*	eel kohm-PLEH-toh
sunglasses	*gli occhiali da sole*	lyee ohk-KYAH-lee dah soh-lay
sweater	*il maglione*	eel mahl-YOH-neh
tie	*la cravatta*	lah krah-VAHT-tah
T-shirt	*la maglietta*	lah mahl-YEHT-tah
umbrella	*l'ombrello*	lohm-BREHL-loh
underwear	*la biancheria intima*	lah byahn-keh-REE-ah een-tee-mah
velvet	*il velluto*	eel vehl-LOO-toh
wallet	*il portafoglio*	eel pohr-tah-FOHL-yoh
wool	*la lana*	lah lah-nah
zipper	*la cerniera*	lah chehr-NYEH-rah

Jewelry

amber	*l'ambra*	lahm-brah
bracelet	*il braccialetto*	eel brah-chah-LEHT-toh
brooch	*la spilla*	lah speel-lah
costume jewelry	*la bigiotteria*	lah bee-joht-teh-REE-ah
cufflinks	*i gemelli da camicia*	ee jeh-MEHL-lee dah kah-MEECH-ah
diamond	*il diamante*	eel dee-ah-MAHN-teh
earrings	*gli orecchini*	lyee ohr-rehk-KEE-nee
emerald	*lo smeraldo*	loh smeh-RAHL-doh
gold	*l'oro*	loh-roh
gold plated	*dorato*	doh-RAH-toh

jewelry	*i gioielli*	ee joy-EHL-lee
necklace	*la collana*	lah koh-LAH-nah
pearls	*le perle*	leh pehr-leh
pendant	*il ciondolo*	eel CHOHN-doh-loh
pin	*lo spillo*	loh-speel-loh
ring	*l'anello*	lah-NEHL-loh
ruby	*il rubino*	eel roo-BEE-noh
sapphire	*lo zaffiro*	loh zahf-FEE-roh
silver	*l'argento*	lahr-JEHN-toh
silver plated	*argentato*	ahr-jehn-TAH-toh
watch	*l'orologio*	loh-roh-LOH-joh
wedding ring	*la fede*	lah feh-deh

Useful Verbs

to button up	*abbottonare*	ahb-boht-toh-NAH-ray
to change, to get changed	*cambiarsi*	kahm-BYAHR-see
to dress (oneself), to get dressed	*vestirsi*	vehs-TEER-see
to fit; to suit	*stare bene (a)*	stah-ray behn-ay ah
to knot, to tie	*annodare*	ahn-nohd-AH-ray
to measure	*misurare*	mee-zoo-RAH-ray
to mend, to repair; to darn	*rammendare*	rahm-mehn-DAH-ray
to sew	*cucire*	koo-CHEE-ray
to take off, to remove	*togliere*	TOHL-yeh-ray
to try	*provare*	proh-vah-ray
to unbutton, to undo	*sbottonare*	sboht-toh-NAH-ray
to undress (oneself), to get undressed	*spogliarsi*	spohl-YAHR-see

Useful Adjectives: Colors

Remember that colors are adjectives and therefore must agree in number and gender with the nouns they modify.

attractive	*attraente*	aht-trah-EHN-teh
black	*nero*	neh-roh
(dark) blue	*blu*	bloo
(pale) blue	*azzurro*	ahds-ZOO-roh
brown	*marrone*	mahr-ROH-neh
comfortable	*comodo*	KOH-moh-doh
elegant	*elegante*	eh-leh-GAHN-teh
fashionable, in fashion	*alla/di moda*	ahl-lah moh-dah
gold (in color), golden	*d'orato*	doh-RAH-toh
(made) of gold, gold	*d'oro*	doh-roh
gray	*grigio*	gree-joe
green	*verde*	vehr-day
long	*lungo*	loon-goh
naked, bare, nude	*nudo*	noo-doh
orange	*arancione*	ah-rahn-CHOH-nay
pink	*rosa*	roh-zah
purple, violet	*viola*	vyoh-lah
red	*rosso*	rohs-soh
rough, coarse	*rozzo*	rohts-soh
short	*corto*	kohr-toh
silver (in color), silvery	*argenteo*	ahr-jehn-TAY-oh
(made) of silver, silver	*d'argento*	dahr-JEHN-toh
soft, smooth	*morbido*	MOHR-bee-doh
thick	*spesso*	spehs-soh
tight(-fitting)	*stretto*	streht-toh
white	*bianco*	byahn-koh
worn out	*consumato*	kohn-soo-MAH-toh
yellow	*giallo*	jahl-loh

Useful Adjectives: Sizes

Shoe and clothing sizes in Europe are different than those used in the United States. Be prepared that the shoe salesman may tell you that you have a size 43 foot.

What size do you wear?
Quale misura desidera?
kwah-lay mee-ZOO-rah deh-zee-deh-rah

I would like . . .
Desidero . . .
deh-zee-deh-roh . . .

I don't know the sizes in Italian.
Non conosco le misure italiane.
nohn koh-NOHS-koh leh mee-zoo-reh ee-tahl-YAHN-eh

It's too big/small.
È troppo grande/piccolo.
eh trohp-poh grahn-day/PEEK-koh-loh

Clothing Size (*la taglia/la misura*)

large	*grande*	grahn-day
larger	*più grande*	pyou grahn-day
medium	*medio*	mehd-ee-oh
small	*piccolo*	PEEK-koh-loh
smaller	*più piccolo*	pyou peek-koh-loh

Chapter 9

Out on the Town

To experience Italy, you have to be tuned in to the culture. If you'd like to get out to a soccer game or perhaps go to the theater, this chapter introduces you to vocabulary and terms related to sports, pastimes, games, and cultural activities.

Sports and Games

Soccer, by far the most popular sport in Italy (and most other countries in the world!), is by no means the only sport in Italy. You will find numerous sports and games available for your recreational pleasure.

Commonly Heard Words

Some words are common to all sports and games. Whether you're reading the newspaper, watching on television, or observing from the audience, you're bound to hear the following words sooner or later.

ball	il pallone	eel pahl-LOH-neh
championship	il campionato	eel kahm-pee-oh-NAH-toh
competition	la gara	lah gah-rah
defeat	la sconfitta	lah skohn-FEET-tah
to enjoy oneself	divertirsi	dee-vehr-TEER-see
entertaining	divertente	dee-vehr-TEHN-tay
entertainment	il divertimento	eel dee-vehr-tee-MEHN-toh
fan	il tifoso	eel tee-FOH-soh
free time	il tempo libero	eel tehm-poh LEE-beh-roh
game	la partita	lah pahr-TEE-tah
to lose	perdere	PEHR-deh-ray
player	il giocatore	eel joh-kah-TOH-ray
popular	popolare	poh-poh-LAH-ray
to prefer	preferire	preh-feh-REE-ray
race	la gara	lah gah-rah
spectators	gli spettatori	lyee speht-tah-TOH-ree
sport	lo sport	loh sport
team	la squadra	lah skwah-drah
victory	la vittoria	lah veet-TOH-ree-ah
to win	vincere	VEEN-cheh-ray

The Verbs *Fare* and *Giocare*

The verb *fare* (to do, to make) can prove very useful when talking about sports and games. *Faccio lo sci nautico* can translate as "I am waterskiing (right now)" or "I waterski (in general)." In the present tense the verb *fare* is irregular.

fare (to do, to make)

io faccio	ee-oh fah-choh
tu fai	tu feye (like the English "eye")
lui, lei, Lei fa	loo-ee, lay fah
noi facciamo	noy fah-CHAH-moh
voi fate	voy fah-tay
loro, Loro fanno	loh-roh fahn-noh

Io faccio . . .

l'alpinismo	mountain climbing
	lahl-pee-NEEZ-moh
la caccia	hunting
	lah kah-chah
il campeggio	camping
	eel kahm-PEHJ-joh
il canotaggio	rowing
	eel kah-noh-TAHJ-joh
il ciclismo	bicycling
	eel chee-KLEEZ-moh
la corsa	auto racing
automobilistica	lah kohr-sah ohw-toh-moh-bee-LEES-tee-kah
la corsa nautica	boat racing
	lah kohr-sah NOHW-tee-kah
l'equitazione	horseback riding
	leh-kwee-tahts-YOH-neh

l'excursionismo	hiking
	lehk-skoor-zee-oh-NEEZ-moh
il footing	jogging
	eel footing
la ginnastica	gymnastics
	lah jeen-NAHS-tee-kah
il gioco dei birilli	bowling
	eel joh-koh day bee-REEL-lee
gli sport	sports
	lyee sport
il nuoto	swimming
	eel noo-OH-toh
la pallamano	handball
	lah pahl-lah-MAH-noh
la pallanuoto	water polo
	lah pahl-lah-noo-OH-toh
la pallavolo	volleyball
	lah pahl-lah-VOH-loh
il patinaggio	skating
	eel pah-tee-NAHJ-joh
il pugilato	boxing
	eel poo-jee-LAH-toh
lo sci di discesa	downhill skiing
	loh shee dee dee-SHAY-zah
lo sci di fondo	cross-country skiing
	loh shee dee fohn-doh
lo sci nautico	waterskiing
	loh shee NOHW-tee-koh

-ALERT

> Golf has become increasingly more popular over the past few years in Italy. Golf courses are widely available, but greens fees can be expensive. Driving ranges are also available, and they offer an inexpensive way to keep your swing in top form!

The verb *giocare* (to play) is usually used when referring to the name of a sport or game. *Gioco a calcio* means "I play soccer." Note that the verb *giocare* takes the preposition *a* when followed by the name of the sport or game.

giocare (to play)

io gioco	ee-oh joh-koh
tu giochi	too joh-kee
lui, lei, Lei gioca	loo-ee, lay joh-kah
noi giochiamo	noy johk-YAH-moh
voi giocate	voy joh-KAH-tay
loro, Loro giocano	loh-roh JOH-kah-noh

Io gioco a . . .

baseball	bayz-ball	baseball
biliardi	beel-YAHR-dee	pool
bocce	boh-cheh	bocce ball
calcio	kahl-choh	soccer
carte	kahr-teh	cards
dardi	dahr-dee	darts
golf	golf	golf

football	foot-ball	American football
americano	ah-meh-ree-KAH-noh	
nascondino	nahs-kohn-DEE-noh	hide-and-seek
pallacanestro	pahl-lah-kah-NES-troh	basketball
pallamano	pahl-lah-MAH-noh	handball
pallavolo	pahl-lah-VOH-loh	volleyball
pallone	pahl-LOH-neh	ball
scacchi	skah-kee	chess
tennis	tennis	tennis

 -ALERT

Italy's national sport, soccer, has a large following throughout the Italian peninsula. If you're visiting Italy in soccer season (which never seems to end!), try to catch a game. Almost all large cities have a professional team, and you'll find semiprofessional and amateur games everywhere.

Soccer

For the uninitiated, soccer can be confusing. The following are some terms you might come across when watching a soccer match:

bicycle kick	*la rovesciata*
	lah roh-veh-SHAH-tah
to cheat	*barare*
	bah-RAH-ray
corner flag	*la bandierina d'angolo*
	lah bahn-dyeh-REE-nah DAHN-goh-loh

crossbar	*la traversa* lah trah-VEHR-sah
dribble	*il dribbling* eel dreeb-bleeng
field	*il campo di calcio* eel kahm-poh dee kahl-choh
foul	*il fallo* eel fahl-loh
free kick	*il calcio di punizione* eel kahl-choh dee poo-neets-YOH-nay
goalkeeper	*il portiere* eel pohr-TYEH-reh
goal kick	*il calcio di rinvio* eel kahl-choh dee reen-vyoh
goal line	*la linea di fondo* lah LEE-neh-ah dee fohn-doh
halfway line	*la linea di metà campo* lah LEE-neh-ah dee meh-TAH kahm-poh
header	*il colpo di testa* eel kohl-poh dee tess-tah
to kick	*calciare* kahl-CHAH-ray
linesman	*il guardalinee* eel gwahr-dah-LEE-neh-eh
midfield player	*il centrocampista* eel chehn-troh-kahm-PEES-tah
obstruction	*l'ostruzione* lohs-troots-YOH-nay
offside	*il fuorigioco* eel fwoh-ree-JOH-koh
pass	*il passaggio* eel pahs-SAHJ-joh

penalty area	*l'area di rigore*
	lah-reh-ah dee ree-goh-ray
post	*il palo*
	eel pah-loh
referee	*l'arbitro*
	LAHR-bee-troh
to score a goal	*fare un gol*
	fah-ray oon gohl
shirt (jersey)	*la maglia*
	lah mahl-yah
short pass	*il passaggio corto*
	eel pahs-SAHJ-joh kohr-toh
sweeper	*il libero*
	eel LEE-beh-roh
throw-in	*la rimessa laterale*
	lah ree-MEHS-sah lah-teh-rah-lay
tie score	*il pareggio*
	eel pah-REHJ-joh
touch line	*la linea laterale*
	lah LEE-neh-ah lah-teh-RAH-lay

Ⓔ-ALERT

In Italian, there are two words (used interchange-ably) for soccer: *il calcio* and *il football*. Football as we know it in the United States is called *football americano* in Italy. When friends want to get together for a pickup game, they will often to refer to it as *pallone* (similar to the way Americans say "Let's play some ball.").

Hobbies

What to do with all your free time? Here's a short list of some hobbies and pastimes practiced throughout the world:

art	*l'arte*	lahr-teh
art exhibit	*la mostra d'arte*	lah mohs-trah dahr-teh
ballet	*il balletto*	eel bahl-LEHT-toh
book	*il libro*	eel lee-broh
cinema	*il cinema*	eel CHI-neh-mah
crossword puzzle	*il cruciverba*	eel kroo-chee-VEHR-bah
to dance	*ballare*	bahl-LAH-ray
dancing	*il ballo*	eel bahl-loh
to draw	*disegnare*	dee-zen-YAH-ray
drawing	*il disegno*	eel dee-ZEHN-yoh
horse racing	*l'ippica*	LEEP-pee-kah
to listen to music	*ascoltare*	ah-skohl-TAH-ray
	la musica	lah MOO-zee-kah
literature	*la letteratura*	lah leht-teh-rah-TOO-rah
novel	*il romanzo*	eel roh-MAHN-zoh
opera	*l'opera*	LOH-peh-rah
to paint	*dipingere*	dee-PEEN-jeh-ray
paintbrush	*il pennello*	eel pehn-NEHL-loh
painting	*la pittura*	lah peet-TOO-rah
pasttime	*il passatempo*	eel pahs-sah-TEHM-poh
photography	*la fotografia*	lah foh-toh-grah-FEE-ah
poetry	*la poesia*	lah poh-eh-ZEE-ah
to read	*leggere*	LEHJ-jeh-ray
sculpture	*la scultura*	lah skool-TOO-rah
theater	*il teatro*	eel teh-AH-troh

Live Performances

Italy has a rich history of performance art. From opera to theater to live concerts, you're bound to find something that appeals to you.

Theater and Opera

Many of Italy's cities have world-class opera houses and theaters. If time is on your side, be sure to book your tickets well in advance—tickets for *La Scala* performances sell out years in advance!

accompanist	*l'accompagnatore* lahk-kohm-pahn-yah-TOH-ray
act	*l'atto* laht-toh
to act	*recitare* reh-chee-TAH-ray
coat check room	*il guardaroba* eel gwahr-dah-ROH-bah
comedy	*la commedia* lah kohm-MEH-dee-ah
conductor	*il direttore d'orchestra* eel dee-reht-TOH-ray dohr-KEHS-trah
costumes	*i costumi* ee kohs-TOO-mee
curtain	*il sipario* eel seep-AH-ree-oh
dancer	*il ballerino* eel bahl-leh-REE-noh
drama	*il dramma* eel drahm-mah
dress rehearsal	*la prova generale* lah proh-vah jeh-neh-RAH-lay

duet	*il duetto*
	eel doo-EHT-toh
to improvise	*improvvisare*
	eem-proh-vee-ZAH-ray
intermission	*l'intervallo*
	leen-tehr-VAHL-loh
lobby	*l'ingresso*
	leen-GREHS-soh
orchestra	*l'orchestra*
	lohr-KESS-trah
overture	*il preludio*
	eel preh-LOO-dyoh
part	*la parte*
	lah pahr-tay
performance	*la rappresentazione*
	lah rahp-preh-zehn-tahts-YOH-nay
producer	*il produttore*
	eel proh-doot-TOH-ray
production	*la messa in scena*
	lah mehs-sah een sheh-nah
program	*il programma*
	eel proh-GRAHM-mah
scenery	*lo scenario*
	loh sheh-NAH-ree-oh
stage	*il palcoscenico*
	eel pahl-koh-SHEH-nee-koh
ticket	*il biglietto*
	eel beel-YEHT-toh
title	*il titolo*
	eel tee-toh-loh
tragedy	*la tragedia*
	lah trah-JEH-dee-ah

Concerts

From the symphony to rock and pop, Italy has it all. Try to take in a show of an Italian artist—music is a great way to learn the language!

to applaud, to clap	*applaudire*	ahp-plohw-DEE-ray
applause	*l'applauso*	lahp-plohw-zoh
cello	*il violoncello*	eel vee-oh-leen-CHEH-loh
chorus	*il coro*	eel koh-roh
clarinet	*il clarinetto*	eel klah-ree-NEHT-toh
classical music	*la musica classica*	lah MOO-zee-kah KLAHS-see-kah
concert	*il concerto*	eel kohn-CHEHR-toh
drums	*la batteria*	lah baht-teh-REE-ah
flute	*il flauto*	eel flohw-toh
guitar	*la chitarra*	lah-kee-TAHR-rah
instrument	*lo strumento*	loh stroo-MEHN-toh
jazz	*il jazz*	eel jehts
to listen (to)	*ascoltare*	ahs-kohl-TAH-ray
oboe	*l'oboe*	LOH-boh-eh

opera	*l'opera*
	LOH-peh-rah
orchestra	*l'orchestra*
	lohr-KEHS-trah
piano	*il pianoforte*
	eel pyah-noh-FOHR-teh
to play by ear	*suonare a orecchio*
	swoh-NAH-ray ah oh-REHK-kyoh
to play by sight	*suonare a prima vista*
	swoh-NAH-ray ah pree-mah vees-tah
to play the guitar	*suonare la chitarra*
	swoh-NAH-ray lah kee-TAHR-rah
to play the piano	*suonare il pianoforte*
	swoh-NAH-ray eel pyah-noh-FOHR-teh
rock music	*la musica rock*
	lah MOO-zee-kah rock
saxophone	*il sassofono*
	eel sahs-SOH-foh-noh
show	*lo spettacolo*
	loh speht-TAH-koh-loh
to sing	*cantare*
	kahn-tah-ray
singer	*il cantante*
	eel kahn-TAHN-tay
song	*la canzone*
	lah kahn-TSOH-nay
stage	*il palcoscenico*
	eel pahl-koh-SHEH-nee-koh
trombone	*il trombone*
	eel trohm-BOH-neh
trumpet	*la tromba*
	lah trohm-bah
violin	*il violino*
	eel vee-oh-LEE-noh

biancheria intima	underwear
bianco	white
bicchiere	glass
bicchiere di succo d'arancia	glass of orange juice
bicicletta	bicycle
bigiotteria	costume jewelry
biglietteria	ticket office
biglietto	ticket
biglietto andata e ritorno	round-trip ticket
biglietto solo andata	one-way ticket
biliardi	pool
bimbo, bimba	baby
binari	tracks
binario	platform
biologo	biologist
biondo	blonde
birra	beer
bischero	stupid person (Tuscany)
biscotto	cookie
bistecca	steak
blu	blue (dark)
bocca	mouth
bocce	bocce ball
bollettino meteorologico	weather report
bollitore	kettle
borsa	handbag
bottiglia	bottle

bottone	button
braccialetto	bracelet
braccio	arm
brasiliano	Brazilian
bravo	good, able
brocca per vino	wine jug
bruciore di stomaco	heartburn
bruno	dark-haired
brutto	ugly
buca delle lettere	mailbox
Buon giorno.	Good day.
Buona mattina.	Good morning.
Buona notte.	Goodnight.
Buona sera.	Good evening.
buono	good
burro	butter
busta paga	pay envelope
cabina telefonica	telephone booth
caccia	hunting
cadere	to fall
caffè	coffee
caffettiera	coffeemaker
calcagno	heel
calciare	to kick
calcio	soccer
calcio di punizione	free kick
calcio di rinvio	goal kick
calcolatrice	pocket calculator

caldo	hot	**capelli secchi**	dry hair
calendario da parete	wall calendar	**capire**	to understand
		capogiro	dizziness
calza	stocking	**capotreno**	chief conductor
calzatura	footwear	**cappello**	hat
calzini	socks	**cappotto**	overcoat
cambiarsi	to change, to get changed	**caraffa per acqua**	water jug
cambio	change	**carciofo**	artichoke
camera	room	**carello**	cart
camera da letto	bedroom	**carie**	cavities
cameriera	waitress	**carne**	meat
cameriere	waiter	**caro**	dear
camicetta	blouse	**carotta**	carrot
camicia	shirt	**carrozza**	car
caminetto	fireplace	**carrozza ristorante**	restaurant car
camino	chimney		
camion	truck	**carta**	paper
campeggio	camping	**carta d'imbarco**	boarding pass
campionato	championship	**carta da pareti**	wallpaper
campo di calcio	soccer field	**carta da visita**	business card
Canada	Canada	**carta igienica**	toilet paper
canadese	Canadian	**carte**	cards
cancello	gate	**cartelda da scrittoio**	blotter
candeggina	bleach		
canino	cuspid	**cartella**	folder
canotaggio	rowing	**cartella sistema**	system folder
cantante	singer	**cartoleria**	paper store
cantare	to sing	**cartolina postale**	postcard
canzone	song		
capelli grassi	oily hair	**casa**	house; home
capelli	hair	**casella posta elettronica**	inbox

casella postale	post office box
casino	mess
cassa	cash register
cassa	teller window
cassettiera	set of drawers
cassetto	drawer
cassetto della scrivania	desk drawer
cassettone	chest of drawers
cassiera	cashier
cassiere	bank teller
cattedrale	cathedral
cattivo	bad
caviglia	ankle
cavolo	cabbage
C'è il sole.	It's sunny.
C'è la nebbia.	It's foggy.
celibe (m.), nubile (f.)	single
cena	dinner
centrocampista	midfield player
cerniera	zipper
cerotto	adhesive bandage
cervello	brain
cestino	wastepaper basket
che	what
Che barba!	How boring!
Che macello!	What a mess!
Che noia!	How boring!
Che roba!	I can't believe it!

Che schifo!	How disgusting!
Che ti passa per la testa?	What's the matter with you?
chi	who
chiamare, telefonare a	to call
chiamarsi	to be called
chiave	key
chiesa	church
chirurgo	surgeon
chitarra	guitar
chiudere	to close, to shut
chiudere il becco	to shut up, to shut one's trap
chiudere le tende	to close/shut the curtains
chiuso	closed
Ci mancherebbe altro!	God forbid!
Ci vediamo . . .	See you . . .
Ci vuole altro!	It takes much more than that!
Ciao!	Hi! (informal)
ciclismo	bicycling
ciliegia	cherry
Cina	China
cinema	cinema
cinese	Chinese
cintura	belt
cintura di sicurezza	seatbelt
ciocca di capelli	wisp of hair
cioccolato	chocolate

ciondolo	pendant		compiti	homework
ciotola	bowl		completo	suit
cipolla	onion		computer	computer
clarinetto	clarinet		con	with
clavicola	collarbone		con bagno	shower in the room
cliccare	to click			
clima	climate		con contanti	in cash
climatizzatore	air conditioning		con i travelers check	with traveler's checks
clinica odontoiatrica	dental clinic		con la carta di credito	with a credit card
cofano	car hood			
cognata	sister-in-law		concerto	concert
cognato	brother-in-law		congelamento	frostbite
cognome	last name		congelatore	freezer
colazione	breakfast		coniglio	rabbit
collana	necklace		consegna bagagli	baggage check
collo	neck		consegnare i bagagli	to check bags
colore	color			
colpo di pistolla	gunshot		consumato	worn out
colpo di testa	header		contabile	accountant
coltello	knife		conto	check/bill
come	how		contorno	vegetable course
Come si chiama Lei?	What's your name? (formal)		contratto	contract
			controllo di sicurezza	security check
Come stai?	How are you?		controllore	conductor
Come ti chiami?	What's your name? (informal)		coperta	blanket
			coperto	cover charge
commedia	comedy		coro	chorus
comodo	comfortable		corona	crown
compagnia aerea	airline		corpo	body

corridoio	corridor, hallway
corsa automobilistica	auto racing
corsa nautica	boat racing
corsia	lane
corso	course
corto	short
costola	rib
costruire	to build, to construct
costume da bagno	bathing suit
costumi	costumes
cotonare	to tease
cotone	cotton
cranio	skull
cravatta	tie
credenza	sideboard
credenza	buffet
crepuscolo	dusk
crisantemo	chrysanthemum
cruciverba	crossword puzzle
cuccetta	sleeping compartment
cucchiaino	teaspoon
cucchiaio	spoon
cucina	kitchen
cucina a gas	gas stove
cucina elettrica	electric stove
cucinare	to cook
cucire	to sew

cuocere	to cook
cugino, cugina	cousin
cuoco/chef	cook (noun)
cuoio	leather
cuore	heart
curriculum	resume
cuscino	pillow
CV	resume
d'accordo	okay
d'orato	gold (in color), golden
da	from, by
da morire	a lot
dal dentista	at the dentist's office
dalia	dahlia
d'altro canto	on the other hand
dardi	darts
dare la precedenza	to yield
dare una multa	to give a ticket
d'argento	silver, made of silver
davanti	in front
davanti a	in front of
Davvero?	Really?
decapotabile	convertible
decollare	to take off
deluvione	flood
denaro/soldi	money
dente	tooth

dente del giudizio	wisdom tooth	**dimettere dall'ospedale**	discharge
dentiera	denture	**dipingere**	to paint
dentifricio	toothpaste	**diploma**	diploma (high school)
dentista	dentist		
dentro	inside, indoors	**direttore d'orchestra**	conductor
dessert/dolce	dessert		
destinatario	addressee	**direttore medico**	medical director
destinazione	destination	**dirigente**	boss, manager
destra	right (direction)	**disegnare**	to draw
di (d')	of, from	**disegno**	drawing
Di dove sei?	Where are you from?	**disinfettante**	disinfectant
		disoccupato	unemployed
di moda	fashionable, in fashion	**disoccupazione**	unemployment
diabete	diabetes	**distributore di benzina**	gas station
diabetico	diabetic	**distributore francobolli**	stamp machine
diagnosi	diagnosis		
diagramma della temperatura	temperature chart	**distributore monete**	coin changer
		dito	finger
diamante	diamond	**divano**	couch, sofa
dicembre	December	**divertente**	entertaining
dichiarazione del valore	value declaration	**divertimento**	entertainment
		divertirsi	to enjoy oneself
dichiarazione doganale	customs declaration	**divorziato(a)**	divorced
		dizionario	dictionary
diesel	diesel	**doccia**	shower
dietro	behind, in back of	**dogana**	customs
		dolci	sweets, dessert
digestivo	after-dinner drink, digestive tonic	**dollaro**	dollar
		dolore	pain
		domani	tomorrow

domenica	Sunday
dorato	gold plated
dormire	to sleep
d'oro	golden, made of gold
dottorato	doctorate degree
dottore/ dottoressa	doctor
dove	where
Dov'è . . . ?/Dove sono . . . ?	Where is . . . ?/ Where are . . . ?
dramma	drama
dribbling	dribble
due letti	two beds
due notti	two nights
due persone	two people
duetto	duet
e	and
economista	economist
edicola, giornalaio	newsstand
egiziano	Egyptian
elegante	elegant
elenco telefonico	phonebook
entrata	entrance
equitazione	horseback riding
erba	grass
erbaccia	weed
esame	test
espresso	special delivery
essere	to be
essere al verde	to be broke

essere in gioco	to be at stake
essere nelle nuvole	to daydream, to have one's head in the clouds
essere un po' di fuori	to be out of one's mind
est	east
estate	summer
estrarre	to pull out, remove
etto	hectogram
euro	the euro
europeo	European
excursionismo	hiking
Fa bel tempo.	It's nice.
Fa caldo.	It's hot.
Fa freddo.	It's cold.
fa presente che	bear in mind
fagioli	beans
fallo	foul
fannullone	lazy bum
fare	to do, to make
fare attenzione	to pay attention
fare benzina	to get gas
fare caldo	to be hot (weather)
fare colazione	to have breakfast
fare freddo	to be cold (weather)
fare i capelli	to do someone's hair
fare il bagno	to take a bath
fare il biglietto	to buy a ticket

fare il bucato	to do the wash/laundry	fare una prenotazione	to make a reservation
fare il grande	to show off	fare una raccomandata	register
fare il numero	to dial the number	fare una radiografia	to x-ray
fare il pieno	to fill it up	fari	lights
fare impazzire	to drive someone crazy	faringite	sore throat
fare l'autostop	to hitchhike	farmacia	pharmacy
fare la barba/radere	to shave	farmacista	pharmacist
fare la doccia	to take a shower	fatti gli affari tuoi	mind your business
fare la guerra	to wage war	febbraio	February
fare la permanente	to perm	febbre	fever
fare la spesa	to go food shopping	fede	wedding ring
		fegato	liver
fare le spese	to go shopping	felice	happy
fare un bagno	to take a bath	ferita	wound
fare un errore	to make a mistake	fermaglio	paper clip
fare un giro	to go for a ride	fermarsi	to stop (oneself)
fare un gol	to score a goal	fermata dell'autobus	bus stop
fare un regalo	to give a gift		
fare un viaggio	to take a trip	ferramenta	hardware store
fare una domanda	to ask a question	ferro da stiro	iron
		ferrovia	railway
fare una foto	to take a picture	fetta di torta	piece of cake
fare una gita	to take a short trip	fidanzata	fiancée
		fidanzato	fiancé
fare una passeggiata	to take a walk	figlia	daughter
		figlio	son
fare una pausa	to take a break	finestra	window
		finestra di dialogo	dialog box

Chapter 10

Italian for Business

Though you will find that many Italians are proficient in English, you will certainly gain the respect of your Italian colleagues by demonstrating a proficiency of your hosts' language. If you're traveling to Italy for business, this chapter will help you make a good impression on your Italian colleagues!

Jobs and Professions

Whatever your profession, a knowledge of a wide variety of professions and jobs can only enhance your business interactions.

accountant	*il contabile*
	eel kohn-TAH-bee-leh
apprentice	*l'apprendista*
	lahp-prehn-DEES-tah
banker	*il banchiere*
	eel ban-KYEH-reh
bank teller	*il cassiere*
	eel kahs-SYEH-reh
biologist	*il biologo*
	eel bee-OH-loh-goh
broker	*il mediatore*
	eel meh-dee-ah-TOH-reh
cashier	*la cassiera*
	lah kahs-SYEH-rah
civil servant	*un impiegato dello stato*
	oon eem-pyeh-GAH-toh dehl-loh stah-toh
dentist	*il dentista*
	eel dehn-TEES-tah
detective	*l'investigatore*
	leen-vehs-tee-gah-TOH-ray
doctor	*il dottore/la dottoressa*
	eel doht-TOH-ray/lah doht-toh-REHS-sah
economist	*l'economista*
	leh-koh-noh-MEES-tah
employee	*l'impiegato*
	leem-pyeh-GAH-toh

engineer	*l'ingegnere*
	leen-jen-YEH-ray
judge	*il giudice*
	eel JOO-dee-cheh
journalist	*il giornalista*
	eel johr-nah-LEES-tah
lawyer	*l'avvocato*
	lahv-voh-KAH-toh
manager	*il dirigente/il manager*
	eel dee-ree-JEHN-tay
notary	*il notaio*
	eel noh-TEYE-oh
nurse	*l'infermiera*
	leen-fehrm-YEH-rah
pharmacist	*il farmacista*
	eel fahr-mah-CHEES-tah
pilot	*il pilota*
	eel pee-LOH-tah
police officer	*il polizotto*
	eel poh-leets-OHT-toh
president	*il presidente*
	eel preh-zee-DEHN-tay
receptionist	*la receptionist*
	lah receptionist
researcher	*il ricercatore*
	eel ree-chehr-kah-TOH-ray
scientist	*lo scienzato*
	loh she-ehn-TSAH-toh
secretary	*la segretaria*
	lah seh-greh-TAH-ree-ah
soldier	*il soldato*
	eel sohl-DAH-toh

stockbroker	*l'agente di cambio*
	lah-JEHN-tay dee kahm-byoh
technician	*il tecnico*
	eel TEHK-nee-koh
writer	*lo scrittore*
	loh skree-TOH-ray

-FACT

Italian business offices are open on Mondays to Fridays from 8:30 A.M. to 1:00 P.M. and again from 3:00 P.M. to 5:00 P.M. Banks are open on Mondays to Fridays from 8:30 A.M. to 1:30 P.M. and from 3:00 P.M. to 4:00 or 5:00 P.M. Stores are open Mondays to Saturdays from 9:00 A.M. to 1:00 P.M. and from 4:30 P.M. to 7:30 P.M.

Italian at Work

Here is an introduction to vocabulary related to white collar professions:

boss, manager	*il dirigente*
	eel dee-ree-JEHN-tay
business card	*la carta da visita*
	lah kahr-tah dah VEE-zee-tah
CEO	*l'amministratore delegato*
	lahm-meen-ee-strah-TOH-ray deh-leh-GAH-toh

company	*l'azienda*
	lahts-YEHN-dah
contract	*il contratto*
	eel kohn-TRAHT-toh
corporate planning	*la programmazione aziendale*
	lah proh-grahm-ahts-YOH-nay
	ahts-yehn-DAH-lay
interview	*l'intervista*
	leen-tehr-VEES-tah
job	*il lavoro*
	eel lah-VOH-roh
meeting	*la riunione*
	lah ree-oon-YOH-nay
pay envelope	*la busta paga*
	lah boos-tah pah-gah
raise	*l'aumento di stipendio*
	lohw-MEHN-toh dee stee-PEHN-dee-oh
resume	*il CV/il curriculum*
	eel chee-vee/eel curriculum
salary	*il salario*
	eel sah-LAH-ree-oh
unemployed	*disoccupato*
	dees-oh-koo-PAH-toh
unemployment	*la disoccupazione*
	lah dees-ohk-oo-pahts-YOH-nay
to hire	*assumere*
	ahs-SOO-meh-ray
to fire	*licenziare*
	lee-chehnts-YAH-ray
to work	*lavorare*
	lah-voh-RAH-ray

-ALERT

Italian workers usually receive their paychecks on a monthly basis (*il mensile*). In December, they normally receive their end of the year bonus, called *la tredicesima* (the thirteenth, as in the thirteenth paycheck of the year), which is equivalent to one month's salary.

On the Phone

One must use the formal way of addressing when conducting business over the phone. To start, you'll need to know that when Italians pick up the phone, they say *Pronto?* (pronounced "prohn-toh").

May I speak to . . . ?
Posso parlare con . . . ?

I would like to speak to . . .
Vorrei parlare con . . .

Who is calling?
Chi parla?

Please hold.
Attenda la linea, per favore.

I'll put you through now.
Glielo passo subito.

I'm sorry, she's/he's not here. Would you like to leave a message?
Mi dispiace, ma non c'è. Vorrebbe lasciare un messaggio?

Terms for Phone Usage

answering machine	*la segreteria telefonica*
	lah seh-greh-teh-REE-ah
	teh-leh-FOH-nee-kah
phonebook	*l'elenco telefonico*
	leh-LEHN-koh teh-lef-FOH-nee-koh
phone number	*il numero di telefono*
	eel NOO-meh-roh dee teh-LEH-foh-noh
to call	*chiamare, telefonare a*
	kyah-MAH-ray, teh-leh-foh-NAH-ray ah
to call back	*richiamare*
	ree-kyah-MAH-ray
to dial the number	*fare il numero*
	fah-ray eel NOO-meh-roh
to hang up	*riattaccare*
	ree-aht-tahk-KAH-ray
to leave a message	*lasciare un messaggio*
	lah-SHAH-ray oon mehs-SAH-joh
to ring	*suonare*
	swoh-NAH-ray

-SSENTIAL

When making a phone call in Italy, try to be as polite as possible, especially if you don't know the person who is answering the phone. You should use the terms *buon giorno*, *per favore*, and *grazie* when necessary.

Office Supplies and Equipment

You need to paperclip some papers together. Now if you only knew the word for paperclip! This section will help you in getting all the supplies you need.

blotter	*la cartella da scrittoio*
	lah kahr-TEHL-lah dah skreet-TOY-oh
cabinet	*l'armadio*
	lahr-MAHD-yoh
clerical assistant	*l'assistente*
	lah-sees-TEHN-teh
clock	*l'orologio*
	loh-roh-LOH-joh
desk	*la scrivania*
	lah skree-vah-NEE-ah
desk drawer	*il cassetto della scrivania*
	eel kahs-SEHT-toh dehl-lah skree-vah-NEE-ah
felt-tip pen	*il pennarello*
	eel pehn-nah-REHL-loh

filing cabinet	*l'armadio per pratiche*
	lahr-MAH-dyoh pehr PRAH-tee-keh
keyboard	*la tastiera*
	lah tahs-TYEH-rah
paperclip	*il fermaglio*
	eel fehr-MAHL-yoh
partition wall	*la parete divisoria*
	lah pah-REH-teh dee-vee-ZOH-ree-ah
pen	*la penna*
	lah pehn-nah
pencil sharpener	*il temperamatite*
	eel tehm-peh-rah-mah-TEE-teh
pocket calculator	*la calcolatrice*
	lah kahl-koh-lah-TREE-cheh
printer	*la stampante*
	lah stahm-PAHN-tay
punch	*il perforatore*
	eel pehr-foh-rah-TOH-ray
ruler	*la riga*
	lah ree-gah
scanner	*lo scanner*
	loh skanner
stapler	*la spillatrice*
	lah speel-lah-TREE-cheh
suspension file	*il raccoglitore delle schede*
	eel rahk-kohl-yah-TOH-ray dehl-leh
	skeh-deh
wall calendar	*il calendario da parete*
	eel kah-lehn-DAH-ree-oh dah pah-REH-
	teh
wastepaper basket	*il cestino*
	eel chehs-TEE-noh

Computers and the Internet

The Internet has forever changed the way the world conducts business. A knowledge of terms related to computing and the Internet will surely be advantageous.

-FACT

> You will find that many English words have found their way into the Italian language. This is especially true with words related to computer technology.

address	*l'indirizzo*
	leen-dee-REETS-soh
browser	*il navigatore*
	eel nah-vee-gah-TOH-ray
to click	*cliccare*
	kleek-KAH-ray
computer	*il computer*
	eel kohm-pyou-tehr
control panel	*il pannello di controllo*
	eel pahn-NEHL-loh dee kohn-TROHL-loh
dialog box	*la finestra di dialogo*
	lah fee-NEHS-trah dee dee-AH-loh-goh
to download	*scaricare*
	skah-ree-KAH-ray
folder	*la cartella*
	lah kahr-TEHL-lah
hyperlink	*l'ipercollegamento*
	lee-pehr-kohl-leh-gah-MEHN-toh
icon	*l'icona*
	lee-KOH-nah

inbox	*la casella di posta elettronica*
	lah kah-ZEHL-lah dee pohs-tah eh-leht-TROH-nee-kah
Internet	*la rete*
	lah reh-teh
keyboard	*la tastiera*
	lah tahs-TYEH-rah
keywords	*le parole chiavi*
	leh pah-ROH-leh kyah-vee
multimedia	*multimediale*
	mool-tee-meh-dee-AH-leh
online	*in linea*
	een LEE-neh-ah
operating system	*il sistema operativo*
	eel sees-TEH-mah oh-peh-rah-TEE-voh
page	*la pagina*
	lah PAH-jee-nah
password	*la parola d'accesso*
	lah pah-ROH-lah dah-CHEHS-soh
printer	*la stampante*
	lah stahm-PAHN-teh
to reboot	*rifare il booting*
	ree-FAH-ray eel boo-teeng
to restart	*riavviare*
	ree-ahv-VYAH-ray
search engine	*il motore di ricerca*
	eel moh-TOH-ray dee ree-CHEHR-kah
site	*il sito*
	eel see-toh
system folder	*la cartella sistema*
	lah kahr-TEHL-lah sees-TEH-mah

In School

Studying abroad in Florence? This section provides some useful words and terms related to high school and college.

-FACT

> The Italian university system differs greatly from its American counterpart. The course of study usually lasts five years in Italy, and many consider the Italian university degree (*la laurea*) to be the equivalent of an American master's degree.

school	*una scuola*
	oo-nah skwoh-lah
high school	*un liceo*
	oon lee-CHEH-oh
university	*un'università*
	oon oo-nee-vehr-see-TAH
backpack	*uno zaino*
	oo-noh dzeye-noh
book	*un libro*
	oon lee-broh
chalk	*un gesso*
	oon jehs-soh
chalkboard	*una lavagna*
	oo-nah lah-VAHN-yah
classroom	*un'aula*
	oon ohw-lah
course	*un corso*
	oon kohr-soh

dictionary	*un dizionario*
	oon deets-yoh-NAH-ree-oh
eraser	*una gomma*
	oo-nah gohm-mah
homework	*i compiti*
	ee KOHM-pee-tee
junior high school	*una scuola media*
	oo-nah skwoh-lah meh-dyah
notebook	*un quaderno*
	oon kwah-DEHR-noh
paper	*la carta*
	lah kahr-tah
piece of paper	*un foglio di carta*
	oon fohl-yoh dee kahr-tah
pen	*una penna*
	oo-nah pehn-nah
pencil	*una mattita*
	oo-nah maht-TEE-tah
test	*un esame*
	oon eh-ZAH-may
diploma (high school)	*un diploma*
	oon dee-PLOH-mah
diploma (university)	*una laurea*
	oo-nah LOHW-reh-ah
doctoral degree	*un dottorato*
	oon doht-toh-RAH-toh

Chapter 11

At the Doctor's Office

Though the hope is that your trip will go off without a hitch, it's possible that you may need to seek a doctor's advice while you're abroad. This chapter contains the words and phrases you might need to know to tell a doctor what's wrong.

Common Ailments and Maladies

This section gives a list of common ailments that can help you to get the help you need. You can use the verb *avere* (to have) with these ailments.

allergy	*l'allergia*
	lahl-lehr-JEE-ah
appendicitis	*l'appendicite*
	lahp-pehn-dee-CHEE-teh
arthritis	*l'artrite*
	lahr-TREE-teh
blood poisoning	*la setticemia*
	lah seht-tee-CHEM-ee-ah
chicken pox	*la varicella*
	lah vah-ree-CHEHL-lah
cold	*il raffreddore*
	eel rahf-frehd-DOH-ray
cough	*la tosse*
	lah tohs-say
diabetes	*il diabete*
	eel dee-ah-BEH-teh
dizziness	*il capogiro*
	eel kah-poh-JEE-roh
fever	*la febbre*
	lah fehb-breh
frostbite	*il congelamento*
	eel kohn-jeh-lah-MEHN-toh
heartburn	*il bruciore di stomaco*
	eel broo-CHOH-ray dee STOH-mah-koh

hypertension	*l'ipertensione*
	lee-pehr-tehns-YOH-nay
insomnia	*l'insonnia*
	leen-SOHN-nee-ah
pain	*il dolore*
	eel doh-LOH-ray
pneumonia	*la polmonite*
	lah pohl-moh-NEE-teh
seasickness	*il mal di mare*
	eel mahl dee mah-ray
sore throat	*la faringite*
	lah fah-rihn-JEE-teh
sprain	*lo strappo muscolare*
	loh strahp-poh moos-koh-LAH-ray
ulcer	*l'ulcera*
	LOOL-cheh-rah
wound	*la ferita*
	lah feh-REE-tah

Another group of illnesses goes with *essere* (to be); for example, "to be diabetic" is *essere diabetico.*

asthmatic	*asmatico*
	ahz-MAH-tee-koh
(having) a cold	*raffreddato*
	rahf-frehd-DAH-toh
diabetic	*diabetico*
	dee-ah-BEH-tee-ko

Here are some useful terms for describing your illness:

to need medicine	*avere bisogno di medicina*
	ah-veh-ray bee-ZOHN-yoh dee
	meh-dee-CHEE-nah
to have high blood	*avere l'ipertensione*
pressure	ah-veh-ray lee-pehr-tehns-YOH-nay
to have low blood	*avere l'ipotensione*
pressure	ah-veh-ray lee-poh-tehns-YOH-nay
to break one's	*rompersi il braccio/la gamba*
arm/leg	ROHM-pehr-see eel brah-choh/
	lah gahm-bah

-ALERT

In Italian, possessive adjectives aren't used with body parts, as in "my nose" or "his arm." Instead, reflexive verbs are used: *Mi fa male la testa* (My head hurts) or *Si è rotto il naso* (He broke his nose).

Parts of the Body

If you have to talk to a doctor, a working knowledge of the geography of the human body will prove helpful.

ankle	*la caviglia*	lah kah-VEEL-yah
arm	*il braccio*	eel brah-choh
armpit	*l'ascella*	lah-SHEHL-lah

artery	*l'arteria*	lahr-teh-REE-ah
body	*il corpo*	eel kohr-poh
bone	*l'osso*	lohs-soh
brain	*il cervello*	eel chehr-VEHL-loh
calf	*il polpaccio*	eel pohl-PAHCH-choh
chest	*il torace*	eel toh-RAH-cheh
collarbone	*la clavicola*	lah klah-VEE-koh-lah
elbow	*il gomito*	eel GOH-mee-toh
finger	*il dito*	eel dee-toh
foot	*il piede*	eel pyeh-deh
hand	*la mano*	lah mah-noh
heart	*il cuore*	eel kwoh-ray
heel	*il calcagno*	eel kahl-KAHN-yoh
hip	*l'anca*	lahn-kah
index finger	*l'indice*	LEEN-dee-cheh
knee	*il ginocchio*	eel jee-NOHK-yoh
larynx	*la laringe*	lah lah-REEN-jeh
leg	*la gamba*	lah gahm-bah
middle finger	*il medio*	eel mehd-yoh
muscle	*il muscolo*	eel MOOS-koh-loh
nail	*l'unghia*	loon-gyah
nerve	*il nervo*	eel nehr-voh
pinkie	*il mignolo*	eel MEEN-yoh-loh
rib	*la costola*	lah KOHS-toh-lah
ring finger	*l'anulare*	lah-noo-LAH-ray
shoulder	*la spalla*	lah spahl-lah
skin	*la pelle*	lah pehl-leh
spine	*la spina dorsale*	lah spee-nah dohr-SAH-lay
stomach	*lo stomaco*	loh STOH-mah-koh
thumb	*il pollice*	eel POHL-lee-cheh
vein	*la vena*	lah veh-nah
wrist	*il polso*	eel pohl-soh

-FACT

When coming up with the plural form of the words for some body parts, you will notice that many of them have irregular plurals: *il dito* becomes *le dita*, *il ginocchio* becomes *le ginocchia*, and *la mano* becomes *le mani*.

The Head

Presented here is a list of terms related to the head, face, ears, eyes, nose, and throat:

cheek	*la guancia*	lah gwahn-chah
chin	*il mento*	eel mehn-toh
ear	*l'orecchio*	loh-REHK-kyoh
eyeball	*il globo oculare*	eel gloh-boh ohk-yoo-LAH-ray
eyebrow	*il sopracciglio*	eel soh-prah-CHEEL-yoh
eyelid	*la palpebra*	lah PAHL-peh-brah
face	*il viso*	eel vee-zoh
forehead	*la fronte*	lah frohn-teh
gum	*la gengiva*	lah jehn-JEE-vah
hair	*i capelli*	ee kah-PEHL-lee
head	*la testa*	lah tess-tah
iris	*l'iride*	LEE-ree-deh
jaw	*la mascella*	lah mah-SHEHL-lah
lip	*il labbro*	eel lahb-broh
mouth	*la bocca*	lah bohk-kah

neck	*il collo*	eel kohl-loh
nose	*il naso*	eel nah-zoh
palate	*il palato*	eel pah-LAH-toh
skull	*il cranio*	eel KRAHN-ee-oh
temple	*la tempia*	lah tehm-pee-ah
throat	*la trachea*	lah trah-keh-ah
tongue	*la lingua*	lah leen-gwah
tonsils	*le tonsille*	leh tohn-SEEL-leh
tooth	*il dente*	eel dehn-teh

Going to the Doctor

If you need to see a doctor while traveling, the following vocabulary, in conjunction with the common ailments section, can help you describe your symptoms.

to be cold	*avere freddo*	freh-doh
to be hot	*avere caldo*	kahl-doh
to be constipated	*avere la stitichezza*	lah stee-tee-KEHTS-sah
to be pregnant	*essere incinta*	een-CHEEN-tah
to be sick	*essere malato*	mah-lah-toh
to be tired	*essere assonnato*	ahs-soh-NAH-toh

If you have an allergy, use the following phrase:

I am allergic to . . .
Sono allergico a . . .
soh-noh ahl-LEHR-jee-koh ah

| aspirin | *l'aspirina* | lahs-pee-REE-nah |
| penicillin | *la penicillina* | lah peh-nee-chee-LEE-nah |

Symptomatic Verbs

to bleed	*sanguinare*	sahn-gwee-NAH-reh
to cough	*tossire*	tohs-SEE-reh
to faint	*svenire*	svehn-EE-reh
to fall	*cadere*	kah-deh-reh
to sneeze	*starnutire*	stahr-noo-TEE-reh
to vomit	*vomitare*	voh-mee-TAH-reh

Going to the Hospital

Hopefully you won't need to visit a hospital, but the following terms may be helpful if you do:

anesthetic	*l'anestitico*
	lah-nes-TEH-tee-koh
blood count	*il quadro ematologico*
	eel kwah-droh eh-mah-toh-LOH-jee-koh
blood test	*l'analisi del sangue*
	lah-NAH-lee-zee dehl sahn-gway
blood transfusion	*la trasfusione di sangue*
	lah trahs-fooz-YOH-neh dee sahn-gway
diagnosis	*la diagnosi*
	lah dee-ahg-NOH-zee
to discharge	*il dimettere dall'ospedale*
	eel dee-MEHT-teh-reh
	dahl-ohs-peh-DAH-leh
doctor	*il dottore*
	eel doht-TOH-reh
examination	*l'analisi*
	lah-NAH-lee-zee
to examine	*visitare*
	vee-zee-TAH-reh

hospital	*l'ospedale*
	lohs-peh-DAH-lay
infusion	*l'infuso*
	leen-FOO-zoh
injection	*l'iniezione*
	leen-yehts-YOH-neh
intensive care unit	*il reparto di cure intensive*
	eel ree-PAHR-toh dee koo-reh
	een-tehn-SEE-veh
medical director	*il direttore medico*
	eel dee-reht-TOH-reh MEH-dee-koh
night nurse	*l'infermiera di notte*
	leen-fehrm-YEH-rah dee noht-tay
nurse	*l'infermiera*
	leen-fehrm-YEH-rah
to operate	*operare*
	oh-peh-RAH-reh
operation	*l'intervento*
	leen-tehr-VEHN-toh
patient	*il paziente*
	eel pahts-YEHN-teh
surgeon	*il chirurgo*
	eel kee-ROOR-goh
temperature chart	*il diagramma della temperatura*
	eel dee-ah-GRAHM-mah dehl-lah tehm-peh-rah-TOO-rah
visiting hours	*l'orario delle visite*
	loh-RAH-ree-oh dehl-leh VEE-zee-teh
to x-ray	*fare una radiografia*
	fah-ray oo-nah rah-dee-oh-grahf-FEE-ah

Going to the Dentist

Though you may find it difficult to talk if you've got a terrible toothache, you may want to familiarize yourself with the following vocabulary—just in case!

at the dentist's office	*dal dentista* dahl dehn-TEES-tah
tooth	*il dente* eel dehn-teh
abscess	*l'ascesso* lah-SHESS-soh
local anesthesia	*l'anestesia locale* lah-nehs-teh-ZEE-ah loh-KAH-lay
molar	*il molare* eel moh-LAH-ray
braces	*l'apparecchio* lahp-pah-REHK-kyoh
bridge	*il ponte* eel pohn-teh
cavities	*le carie* le KAH-ree-eh
crown	*la corona* lah koh-ROH-nah
cuspid	*il canino* eel kah-NEE-noh
dental clinic	*la clinica odontoiatrica* lah KLEE-nee-kah oh-dohn-toy-AH-tree-kah
denture	*la dentiera* lah dehn-TYEH-rah
to extract	*estrarre* ehs-TRAH-ray

false tooth	*la protesi*
	lah PROH-teh-zee
fill	*otturare*
	oht-too-RAH-ray
filling	*l'otturazione*
	loht-too-rahts-YOH-nay
gums	*le gengive*
	leh jehn-JEE-veh
incisor	*l'incisivo*
	leen-chee-ZEE-voh
injection	*l'iniezione*
	leen-yehts-YOH-neh
jaw	*la mascella*
	lah mah-SHEHL-lah
nerve	*il nervo*
	eel nehr-voh
oral surgeon	*l'odontoiatra*
	loh-dohn-toy-AHT-rah
orthodontist	*l'ortodontista*
	lohr-toh-dohn-TEES-tah
plaster cast	*il modello in gesso*
	eel moh-DEHL-loh een jehs-soh
root	*la radice*
	lah rah-DEE-cheh
root canal work	*il trattamento della radice*
	eel traht-tah-MEHN-toh dehl-lah
	rah-DEE-cheh
tartar	*il tartaro*
	eel TAHR-tah-roh
temporary filling	*l'otturazione provvisoria*
	loht-too-rahts-YOH-neh
	prohv-veez-OH-ree-ah

toothache	*il mal di denti*
	eel mahl dee dehn-tee
wisdom tooth	*il dente del giudizio*
	eel dehn-teh dehl joo-DEET-see-oh

-FACT

The Italian preposition *da* does not have an exact translation in English. It is commonly used to mean "at the home/office/place of," as in *dal dentista* (at the dentist's office) and *da Mario* (at Mario's house/place).

A Few Dental Verbs

to bleed	*sanguinare*
	sahn-gwee-NAH-reh
to brush one's teeth	*spazzolarsi i denti*
	spahts-soh-LAHR-see ee dehn-tee
to lose a tooth	*perdere un dente*
	PEHR-deh-reh oon DEHN-teh
to pull out, remove	*estrarre*
	ehs-TRAH-reh
to rinse	*sciacquare*
	shock-WAH-reh

Going to the Pharmacy

The following words will help you get what you need in a
pharmacy. Pharmacies all over Italy can be recognized by
the big green cross above the entrance.

pharmacy	*la farmacia* lah fahr-mah-CHEE-ah
pharmacist	*il farmacista* eel fahr-mah-CHEES-tah
ace bandage	*la benda elastica* lah ben-dah eh-LAHS-tee-kah
adhesive bandage	*il cerotto* eel cheh-ROHT-toh
aspirin	*l'aspirina* lahs-pee-REE-nah
cough syrup	*lo sciroppo per la tosse* loh shee-ROHP-poh pehr lah tohs-seh
digestive tonic	*il digestivo* eel dee-jess-TEE-voh
disinfectant	*il disinfettante* eel dees-een-feht-TAHN-teh
drops	*le gocce* leh goh-cheh
gauze bandage	*la garza* lah gahr-zah
insect repellant	*l'insetticida* leen-seht-tee-CHEE-dah
laxative	*il lassativo* eel lahs-sah-TEE-voh
medicine	*la medicina* lah meh-dee-CHEE-nah
pill	*la pastiglia* lah pahs-TEEL-yah

prescription	*la ricetta*
	lah ree-CHEHT-tah
prophylactics	*i preservativi*
	ee preh-zehr-vah-TEE-vee
remedy	*il rimedio*
	eel ree-MEH-dyoh
thermometer	*il termometro*
	eel tehr-MOH-meh-troh
tranquilizer	*il tranquillante*
	eel trahn-kwee-LAHN-tay
vaseline	*la vaselina*
	lah vah-zeh-LEE-nah

Emergencies and Disasters

It's more than likely you will never need to know any vocabulary relating to emergencies or disasters, but here are a few key words and phrases:

Help!	*Aiuto!*
	ah-YOU-toh
Police!	*Polizia!*
	poh-leets-EE-ah
Thief!	*Al ladro!*
	ahl lah-droh
Watch out!	*Attenzione!*
	aht-tehnts-YOH-neh
accident	*un incidente*
	oon een-chee-DEHN-teh
attack	*un attentato*
	oon aht-tehn-TAH-toh

burglary	*un furto*
	oon foor-toh
fire	*un incendio*
	oon een-CHEHN-dyoh
flood	*una deluvione*
	oo-nah deh-loov-YOH-neh
gunshot	*un colpo di pistolla*
	oon kohl-poh dee pees-TOH-lah
to rape	*violentare*
	vee-oh-lehn-TAH-reh
ambulance	*un'ambulanza*
	oon-ahm-boo-LAHN-zah

Chapter 12

In Your Community

If you plan on staying in Italy for an extended period of time, you will need to take care of the inevitable day-to-day tasks. This chapter will provide you with common terms and expressions for your everyday interactions with shopkeepers and postal employees. Remember, Italians are very receptive to outsiders who make an effort to speak their language!

At the Market

Food shopping in Italy can be a fun and interesting experience. You will find supermarkets (very similar to their American counterparts) pretty much everywhere. Many Italians, however, prefer to shop at local, privately owned specialty shops or perhaps at the local *mercato centrale*.

bakery	*la panetteria*
	lah pah-neht-teh-REE-ah
book shop	*la libreria*
	lah lee-breh-REE-ah
butcher shop	*la macelleria*
	lah mah-chehl-leh-REE-ah
central market	*mercato centrale*
	mehr-KAH-toh chehn-TRAH-leh
dairy	*la latteria*
	lah laht-teh-REE-ah
department store	*il grande magazzino*
	eel grahn-day mah-gahts-SEE-noh
fishmonger	*la pescheria*
	lah pehs-keh-REE-ah
florist	*il fioraio*
	eel fyoh-REYE-oh
green grocer	*il fruttivendolo*
	eel froot-tee-VEHN-doh-loh
grocery store	*un alimentari*
	oon ah-lee-mehn-TAH-ree
hardware store	*la ferramenta*
	lah fehr-reh-MEHN-tah
jewelry store	*la gioielleria*
	lah joy-ehl-leh-REE-ah

newsstand	*il giornalaio* eel johr-nah-LEYE-oh
paper store	*la cartoleria* lah kahr-toh-leh-REE-ah
pastry shop	*la pasticceria* lah pahs-tee-cheh-REE-ah
perfume store	*la profumeria* lah proh-foo-meh-REE-ah
pharmacy	*la farmacia* lah fahr-mah-CHEE-ah
supermarket	*il supermercato* eel soo-pehr-mehr-KAH-toh
toy store	*il negozio di giocattoli* eel neh-GOHT-see-oh dee joh-KAHT-toh-lee

In the Shop

cash register	*la cassa* lah kahs-sah
closed	*chiuso* kyou-zoh
entrance	*l'entrata* lehn-TRAH-tah
exit	*l'uscita* loo-SHEE-tah
sale	*i saldi* ee sahl-dee
special offer	*offerta speciale* ohf-FEHR-tah speh-CHAH-leh
open	*aperto* ah-PEHR-toh
opening hours	*orario di apertura* oh-RAH-ree-oh dee ah-pehr-TOO-rah

-FACT

Larger Italian supermarkets of the chain store variety will charge you a 1€ deposit for a shopping cart, which is returned to you after you've finished your shopping. Also, many supermarkets charge for shopping bags to encourage customers to bring their own bags and reduce waste.

Quantities, Weights, and Measures

Knowing the correct terms for quantities, weights, and measures can be very helpful when you are out shopping for food.

How much does it weigh? It weighs . . . kilograms.
Quanto pesa? Pesa . . . kili.
Kwahn-toh peh-zah   Peh-zah keelee

bit, piece	*un po' di*	oon poh dee
bottle	*bottiglia*	boht-TEEL-yah
box	*scattola*	SKAHT-toh-lah
can	*lattina*	laht-TEE-nah
jar	*barattola*	bah-RAHT-toh-lah
gram	*gramma*	grahm-mah
hectogram	*un etto*	oon eht-toh
kilogram	*un kilo*	oon kee-loh
liter	*litro*	lee-troh

-ALERT

When ordering food items by weight, you are more likely to express that weight using hecto-grams (*etti*). For example, *un etto di prosciutto crudo* would be about 3.5 ounces of prosciutto, a little less than a quarter pound.

enough	*basta*	bahs-tah
more	*ancora*	ahn-KOH-rah
less, fewer	*meno*	may-noh
a little	*un po' di*	oon poh dee
too much, too many	*troppo*	trohp-poh

In the Coffee Shop

There seems to be a coffee shop—in Italian, *il bar*—on every street corner in Italy. It is the place where people go for a quick breakfast or lunch, a cup of coffee, an aperitif, or a quick snack.

a cup of coffee	*un caffè*
	oon kahf-feh
a cup of tea	*un tè*
	oon-teh
a glass of orange juice	*un bicchiere di succo d'arancia*
	oon bee-KYEH-reh dee soo-koh dee
	ah-RAHN-chah
a piece of cake	*una fetta di torta*
	oo-nah feht-tah dee tohr-tah

cake	*la torta*	lah tohr-tah
chocolate	*il cioccolato*	eel choh-koh-LAH-toh
coffee	*il caffè*	
	eel kahf-feh	
cookies	*i biscotti*	
	ee beez-KOHT-tee	
fruit tart	*la torta di frutta*	
	lah tohr-tah dee froot-tah	
ice cream	*il gelato*	
	eel jeh-LAH-toh	
chocolate ice cream	*il gelato al cioccolato*	
	eel jeh-LAH-toh ahl choh-koh-LAH-toh	
strawberry ice cream	*il gelato alla fragola*	
	eel jeh-LAH-toh ahl-lah FRAH-goh-lah	
vanilla ice cream	*il gelato alla vaniglia*	
	eel jeh-LAH-toh ahl-lah vah-NEEL-yah	
lemon sherbet	*il sorbetto al limone*	
	eel sohr-BEHT-toh ahl lee-MOH-neh	
orange sherbet	*il sorbetto all'arancia*	
	eel sohr-BEHT-toh ahl-lah-RAHN-chah	
raspberry sherbet	*il sorbetto ai lamponi*	
	eel sohr-BEHT-toh eye lahm-POH-nee	
sugar	*lo zucchero*	
	loh ZOO-keh-roh	
sweets	*i dolci*	
	ee dohl-chee	
whipped cream	*la panna montata*	
	lah pahn-nah mohn-TAH-tah	

At the Post Office

Le Poste Italiane offers numerous services, including banking services, pension services, bill processing, and, last but not least, postal services. The post office is generally open Monday to Friday from 8:30 A.M. to 7:00 P.M. and on Saturdays from 8:30 A.M. to 1:00 P.M. Summer hours will vary, and there may occasionally be a *chiuso per sciopero* ("closed for strike") sign in the window when there's an important soccer game on television.

address	*l'indirizzo*
	leen-dee-REETS-soh
addressee	*il destinatario*
	eel dehs-tee-nah-TAH-ree-oh
air mail	*la posta aerea*
	lah pohs-tah ah-EH-reh-ah
coin changer	*il distributore monete*
	eel dees-tree-boo-TOH-reh moh-NEH-teh
commemorative	*il francobollo emissione speciale*
stamp	eel frahn-koh-BOHL-loh eh-mees-YOH-
	neh speh-CHAH-leh
counter	*lo sportello*
	loh spohr-TEHL-loh
customs declaration	*la dichiarazione doganale*
	lah dee-kyah-rahts-YOH-neh doh-goh-
	NAH-leh
destination	*la destinazione*
	lah dehs-tee-nahts-YOH-neh
information	*l'informazione*
	leen-fohr-mahts-YOH-neh
letter	*la lettera*
	lah LEHT-teh-rah

mailbox	*la buca delle lettere*
	lah boo-kah dehl-leh LEHT-teh-reh
package	*il pacco*
	eel pahk-koh
postage	*l'affrancatura*
	lahf-frahn-kah-TOO-rah
postal clerk	*l'impiegato postale*
	leem-pyeh-GAH-toh pohs-TAH-leh
postcard	*la cartolina postale*
	lah kahr-toh-LEE-nah pohs-TAH-leh
post office box	*la casella postale*
	lah kah-ZEHL-lah pohs-TAH-leh
postman	*il postino*
	eel pohs-TEE-noh
printed matter	*le stampe*
	leh stahm-peh
receipt	*la ricevuta*
	lah ree-cheh-VOO-tah
to register	*fare una raccomandata*
	fah-ray oo-nah rahk-koh-mahn-DAH-tah
registered letter	*la raccomandata*
	lah rahk-koh-mahn-DAH-tah
sender	*il mittente*
	eel meet-TEHN-teh
small parcel	*il pacchetto*
	eel pahk-KEHT-toh
special delivery	*l'espresso*
	lehs-PRESS-oh
stamp (noun)	*il francobollo*
	eel frahn-koh-BOHL-loh
stamp (verb)	*affrancare*
	ahf-frahn-KAH-reh

stamp machine	*il distributore francobolli*
	eel dees-tree-boo-TOH-reh
	frahn-koh-BOHL-lee
telegram	*il telegramma*
	eel teh-leh-GRAHM-mah
unstamped	*non affrancato*
	nohn ahf-frahn-KAH-toh
value declaration	*la dichiarazione del valore*
	lah dee-kyah-rahts-YOH-neh dehl
	vah-LOH-reh

Weather Words and Expressions

If you're out and about and the weather starts to change, this section will help you come up with the correct words and terms.

How's the weather?
Che tempo fa?
Keh tehm-poh fah

It's sunny.	*C'è il sole.*	cheh eel soh-leh
It's nice.	*Fa bel tempo.*	fah behl tehm-poh
It's cold.	*Fa freddo.*	fah frehd-doh
It's hot.	*Fa caldo.*	fah kahl-doh
It's snowing.	*Nevica.*	NEH-vee-kah
It's raining.	*Piove.*	pyoh-veh
It's windy.	*Tira vento.*	tee-rah vehn-toh
It's foggy.	*C'è la nebbia.*	cheh lah nehb-byah
storm	*il temporale*	eel tehm-poh-RAH-leh
lightning	*il lampo*	eel lahm-poh
changeable	*variabile*	vah-ree-AH-bee-leh

air	*l'aria*	lah-ree-ah
rain	*la pioggia*	lah pyoh-jah
barometer	*il barometro*	eel bah-ROH-meh-troh
to rain	*piovere*	PYOH-veh-reh
blizzard	*la tormenta*	lah tohr-MEHN-tah
snow	*la neve*	lah neh-veh
climate	*il clima*	eel klee-mah
storm	*la tempesta*	lah tehm-PESS-tah
cloud	*la nuvola*	lah noo-voh-lah
sun	*il sole*	eel soh-leh
rainstorm	*il temporale*	eel tehm-poh-RAH-leh
cloudy	*nuvoloso*	noo-voh-LOH-soh
dusk	*il crepuscolo*	eel kreh-POOS-koh-loh
fog	*la nebbia*	lah nehb-byah
frost	*il gelo*	eel jeh-loh
hail	*la grandine*	leh GRAHN-dee-neh
ice	*il ghiaccio*	eel gyah-choh
mist	*la foschia*	lah fohs-kyah
weather report	*il bollettino meteorologico*	eel bohl-leht-TEE-noh meh-tee-oh-roh-LOH-jee-koh

E-ALERT

Italy's weather tends to be more moderate than the frigid winters and hot and humid summers in some parts of the United States. Many people consider the spring (April and May) and autumn (September and October) to be the best times to visit Italy. The weather is mild and there are fewer tourists at these times.

Chapter 13

Italian at Home

Practicing Italian at home can be a good way to prepare for your trip. Use sticky notes to label items in your house, and try to remember some useful terms and phrases. Try teaching some words to your family members so you can quiz each other. It can only help!

Things to Do at Home

You've learned a lot of words and expressions related to travel. Now take a look at some useful verbs that have to do with life at home. Many of them are verbs; see Chapter 2 to review how to conjugate verbs.

to build, to construct	*costruire*	kohs-troo-EE-ray
to clean	*pulire*	poo-LEE-ray
to clean/brush one's teeth	*lavarsi i denti*	lah-VAHR-see ee dehn-tee
to close, to shut	*chiudere*	KYEW-deh-ray
to close/shut the curtains	*chiudere le tende*	KYEW-deh-ray leh tehn-deh
to cook	*cucinare*	koo-chee-NAH-ray
to comb one's hair	*pettinarsi*	peht-tee-NAHR-see
to do the washing/laundry	*fare il bucato*	fah-ray eel boo-KAH-toh
to get up, to rise	*alzarsi*	ahl-TSAHR-see
to go to bed	*andare a letto*	ahn-DAH-ray ah leht-toh
to go to sleep; to fall asleep	*addormentarsi*	ahd-dohr-mehn-TAHR-see
to hang up the washing/laundry	*stendere il bucato*	STEHN-deh-ray eel boo-KAH-toh
to iron	*stirare*	stee-RAH-ray
to lie down	*sdraiarsi*	sdreye-AHR-see
to open	*aprire*	ahp-REE-ray
to open/draw the curtains	*aprire le tende*	ahp-REE-ray leh tehn-deh
to paint; to varnish	*verniciare*	vehr-nee-CHAH-ray

to repair	*riparare*	ree-pah-RAH-ray
to sit down	*sedersi*	seh-DEER-see
to sleep	*dormire*	dohr-MEE-ray
to take a bath	*fare un bagno*	fah-ray oon bahn-yoh
to take a shower	*fare la doccia*	fah-ray lah doh-chah
to turn/switch on	*accendere*	ah-CHEN-deh-ray
to wash	*lavare*	lah-VAH-ray
to wash (oneself), to wash up	*lavarsi*	lah-VAHR-see

-FACT

In Italian there aren't separate words for house (structure) and home (environment). The distinction is made by using the definite article. *Vado a casa* means "I'm going home"; *Vado alla casa di Paolo* means "I'm going to Paul's house."

Inside Your Home

Here are terms you can use to describe the contents of your home:

Appliances and Electronics

air conditioning	*l'aria condizionata* LAH-ree-ah kohn-deets-ee-oh-NAH-tah
alarm clock	*la sveglia* lah svehl-yah

central heating	*il riscaldamento centrale*
	eel ree-skahl-dah-MEHN-toh chehn-TRAH-lay
computer	*il computer*
	eel kohm-PYOU-tehr
dishwasher	*la lavastoviglie*
	lah lah-vah-stoh-VEEL-yeh
DVD player	*il lettore DVD*
	eel leht-TOH-ray dee-voo-dee
electric socket	*la presa (di corrente)*
	lah pray-zah dee kohr-REHN-tay
electric stove	*la cucina elettrica*
	lah koo-CHEE-nah eh-LEHT-tree-kah
electrical switch	*l'interruttore*
	leen-tehr-root-TOH-ray
freezer	*il congelatore*
	eel kohn-jeh-lah-TOH-ray
gas stove	*la cucina a gas*
	lah koo-CHEE-nah ah gahs
iron	*il ferro da stiro*
	eel fehr-roh dah stee-roh
microwave (oven)	*il forno a microonde*
	eel fohr-noh ah mee-kroh-OHN-deh
oven	*il forno*
	eel fohr-noh
printer	*la stampante*
	lah stahm-PAHN-tay
radio	*la radio*
	lah RAH-dee-oh
refrigerator, fridge	*il frigorifero*
	eel free-goh-REE-feh-roh
telephone	*il telefono*
	eel teh-LEH-foh-noh

television set	*il televisore*	eel teh-leh-vee-ZOH-ray
vacuum cleaner	*l'aspirapolvere*	lah-spee-rah-POHL-veh-ray
VCR	*il videoregistratore*	eel vee-deh-oh-reh-jee-strah-TOH-ray
washing machine	*la lavatrice*	lah lah-vah-TREE-cheh

-SSENTIAL

To practice your Italian, try renting an Italian movie or watching Italian television. Many cable companies in metropolitan areas in the United States offer Italian network television (RAI).

House and Home: Inside

apartment	*l'appartamento*	lahp-pahr-tah-MEHN-toh
armchair	*la poltrona*	lah pohl-TROH-nah
at home	*a casa*	ah kah-zah
attic	*la soffitta*	lah sohf-FEET-tah
balcony	*il balcone*	eel bahl-KOH-nay
bed	*il letto*	eel leht-toh
bedroom	*la camera da letto*	lah KAH-meh-rah dah leht-toh
blanket	*la coperta*	lah koh-PEHR-tah
broom	*la scopa*	lah skoh-pah
bucket	*il secchio*	eel sehk-kyoh

buffet	*la credenza*	lah kreh-DEHN-zah
carpet	*la moquette*	lah moh-keht
ceiling	*il soffitto*	eel sohf-FEET-toh
chair	*la sedia*	lah seh-dyah
chest of drawers	*il cassettone*	eel kahs-seht-TOH-nay
chimney	*il camino*	eel kah-MEE-noh
clean	*pulito*	poo-LEE-toh
closet, wardrobe	*l'armadio*	lahr-MAHD-yoh
cloth, rag	*lo straccio*	loh strahch-choh
couch, sofa	*il divano*	eel dee-VAH-noh
curtain	*la tenda*	lah tehn-dah
desk	*la scrivania*	lah skree-vah-NEE-ah
dining room	*la sala da pranzo*	lah sah-lah dah prahn-zoh
dirty	*sporco*	spohr-koh
door	*la porta*	lah pohr-tah
drawer	*il cassetto*	eel kahs-SEHT-toh
dry	*secco*	sehk-koh
dust	*la polvere*	lah POHL-veh-ray
fireplace	*il caminetto*	eel kah-mee-NEHT-toh
floor	*il pavimento*	eel pah-vee-MEHN-toh
floor, story	*il piano*	eel pyah-noh
furniture	*i mobili*	ee MOH-bee-lee
garbage	*la spazzatura*	lah spahts-sah-TOO-rah
house; home	*la casa*	lah kah-zah
inside, indoors	*dentro*	dehn-troh
key	*la chiave*	lah kyah-vay
living room	*il soggiorno*	eel soh-JOHR-noh

lock	*la serratura*	lah sehr-rah-TOO-rah
pillow	*il cuscino*	eel koo-SHEE-noh
radiator	*il termosifone*	eel tehr-moh-see-FOH-nay
roof	*il tetto*	eel teht-toh
room	*la stanza*	lah stahn-zah
rug, mat	*il tappeto*	eel tahp-PEH-toh
sheets	*le lenzuola*	lah lents-WOH-lah
shelf; bookcase	*lo scaffale*	loh skahf-FAH-lay
shutter	*l'imposta*	leem-POHS-tah
staircase, stairs	*la scala*	lah skah-lah
stool	*lo sgabello*	loh sgah-BEHL-loh
study	*lo studio*	loh STOO-dee-oh
table	*il tavolo*	eel TAH-voh-loh
telephone	*il telefono*	eel teh-LEH-foh-noh
vase	*il vaso*	eel vah-soh
wall	*la parete*	lah pah-REH-teh
wallpaper	*la carta da pareti*	lah kahr-tah dah pah-REH-tee
window	*la finestra*	lah fee-NEHS-trah

-FACT

Italy is a major producer of furniture and housewares. Try to find a furniture store or housewares store—you may just find something to bring home with you.

Bathroom

bath; bathroom	*il bagno*	eel bahn-yoh
bathtub	*la vasca da bagno*	lah vahs-kah dah bahn-yoh
brush	*la spazzola*	lah SPAHT-soh-lah
hairdryer	*il phon*	eel fohn
mirror	*lo specchio*	loh spehk-kyoh
shampoo	*lo shampoo*	loh shahm-poo
shower curtain	*la tenda da doccia*	lah tehn-dah dah doh-chah
shower	*la doccia*	lah doh-chah
sink	*il lavandino*	eel lah-vahn-DEE-noh
soap	*il sapone*	eel sah-POH-nay
toilet	*la toilette*	lah twah-leht
toilet paper	*la carta igienica*	lah kahr-tah ee-JEH-nee-kah
toothbrush	*la spazzola per i denti*	lah SPAHT-soh-lah pehr ee dehn-tee
toothpaste	*il dentifricio*	eel dehn-tee-FREE-choh
towel	*l'asciugamano*	lah-shoo-gah-MAH-noh

Kitchen

burner (stove)	*il fornello*	eel fohr-NEHL-loh
chair	*la sedia*	lah sehd-yah
chandelier	*il lampadario*	eel lahm-pah-DAH-ree-oh
coffeemaker	*la caffettiera*	lah kahf-feht-TYEER-ah
cook	*il cuoco*	eel kwoh-koh
cupboard	*l'armadietto*	lahr-mah-DYET-toh

cup	*la tazza*	lah tahts-sah
dinner plate	*il piatto*	eel pyaht-toh
dishwasher	*la lavastoviglie*	lah lah-vah-stoh-VEEL-yeh
drying rack	*lo scolapiatti*	loh skoh-lah-PYAHT-tee
fork	*la forchetta*	lah fohr-KEHT-tah
freezer	*il congelatore*	eel kohn-jeh-lah-TOH-ray
fridge	*il frigorifero*	eel free-goh-REE-feh-roh
frying pan	*la padella*	lah pah-DEHL-lah
glass	*il bicchiere*	eel beek-YEH-ray
kettle	*il bollitore*	eel bohl-lee-TOH-ray
kitchen	*la cucina*	lah koo-CHEE-nah
knife	*il coltello*	eel kohl-TEHL-loh
napkin	*il tovagliolo*	eel toh-vahl-YOH-loh
oven	*il forno*	eel fohr-noh
salad bowl	*l'insalatiera*	leen-sah-laht-YEH-rah
saucepan	*la pentola*	lah PEHN-toh-lah
set of drawers	*la cassettiera*	lah kahs-seht-TYEH-rah
sideboard	*la credenza*	lah kreh-DEHN-zah
sink	*il lavandino*	eel lah-vahn-DEE-noh
soup bowl	*il piatto fondo*	eel pyaht-toh fohn-doh
spoon	*il cucchiaio*	eel kook-KYEYE-oh (eye like the English word "eye")
tablecloth	*la tovaglia*	lah toh-VAHL-yah
table	*il tavolo*	eel TAH-voh-loh
teaspoon	*il cucchiaino*	eel koo-kyeye-EE-noh

189

to cook	cucinare/	koo-chee-NAH-ray
	cuocere	KWOH-cheh-ray
toaster	il tostapane	eel tohs-tah-PAH-nay
water jug	la caraffa per	lah kah-RAHF-fah
	acqua	pehr ahk-wah
wine jug	la brocca	lah brohk-kah
	per vino	pehr vee-noh

Home and Garden: Outside

fence	il recinto	eel reh-CHEEN-toh
garage	il garage	eel gah-rahj
gate	il cancello	eel kahn-CHEH-loh
grass	l'erba	lehr-bah
hoe	la zappa	lah dzahp-pah
lawn	il prato	eel prah-toh
lawnmower	la tagliaerba	lah tahl-yah-EHR-bah
leaves	le foglie	leh fohl-yeh
outside, outdoors	fuori	fwoh-ree
rake	il rastrello	eel rahs-TREHL-loh
shovel	la pala	lah pah-lah
vegetable garden	l'orto	lohr-toh
weed	l'erbaccia	lehr-BAH-chah
yard, garden	il giardino	eel jahr-DEE-noh

Garden Flowers

azalea	l'azalea	lahts-AH-leh-ah
begonia	la begonia	lah beh-GOH-nyah
carnation	il garofano	eel gah-ROH-fah-noh
chrysanthemum	il crisantemo	eel kree-ZAHN-teh-moh
dahlia	la dalia	lah dah-lyah
daisy	la margherita	lah mahr-geh-REE-tah

fuchsia	*la fucsia*	lah foo-shah
gardenia	*la gardenia*	lah gahr-DEH-nee-ah
geranium	*il geranio*	eel jeh-RAH-nee-oh
gladiolus	*il gladiolo*	eel glah-dee-OH-loh
hibiscus	*l'ibisco*	lee-BEES-koh
hyacinth	*il giacinto*	eel jah-CHEEN-toh
hydrangea	*l'ortensia*	lohr-TEHN-see-ah
jasmine	*il gelsomino*	eel jehl-soh-MEE-noh
lilac	*il lilla*	eel leel-lah
lily	*il giglio*	eel jee-lyoh
magnolia	*la magnolia*	lah mahg-NOH-lyah
mimosa	*la mimosa*	lah mee-MOH-zah
petunia	*la petunia*	lah peh-TOO-nyah
rose	*la rosa*	lah roh-zah
tulip	*il tulipano*	eel too-lee-PAH-noh
wisteria	*il glicine*	eel GLEE-chee-neh
zinnia	*la zinnia*	lah DSEE-nee-ah

-FACT

Plant and flower shows are very popular in Italy.
If it's the right season, ask your hotel concierge if
there's one in town.

Chapter 14

Common Italian Idioms, Expressions, and Slang

Understanding and correctly using idioms, expressions, and slang will help add character to your spoken language. These terms and expressions often don't translate literally from one language to another, and non-native speakers may have difficulty understanding how and when to use them. Try to tune your ear into conversations as you travel—you will find that Italians have many colorful (and amusing!) sayings and expressions for many different situations.

Idiomatic Expressions with the Verbs *Avere*, *Eessere*, *Stare*, and *Fare*

Avere, *essere*, *stare*, and *fare* are commonly used verbs in Italian, and they are often used in idiomatic expressions. The following lists are by no means exhaustive, but they are a good representation of everyday expressions.

Idiomatic Expressions with *Avere*

Avere is an irregular verb in the present tense.

avere fame ah-VEH-ray fahm-ay	to be hungry
avere sete ah-VEH-ray seh-tay	to be thirsty
avere sonno ah-VEH-ray sohn-noh	to be sleepy
avere caldo ah-VEH-ray kahl-doh	to be warm (hot)
avere freddo ah-VEH-ray frehd-doh	to be cold
avere fretta ah-VEH-ray freht-tah	to be in a hurry
avere paura (di) ah-VEH-ray pah-OOH-rah dee	to be afraid (of)
avere bisogno di ah-VEH-ray bee-ZOHN-yoh dee	to need, have need of
avere voglia di ah-VEH-ray vohl-yah dee	to want, to feel like
avere ragione ah-VEH-ray rah-JOH-nay	to be right, correct
avere torto ah-VEH-ray tohr-toh	to be wrong, incorrect

avere un chiodo fisso in testa ah-VEH-ray oon key-OH-doh fees-soh een tehs-tah	to be fixated on something
avere + number + *anni* ah-VEH-ray + ____ + ahn-nee	to be . . . years old
Quanti anni hai? ? kwahn-tee ahn-nee eye	How old are you?
Ho trentadue anni. oh trehn-tah-DOO-eh ahn-nee	I'm thirty-two years old.

Idiomatic Expressions with *Essere*

Though not as common as idiomatic expressions with *avere*, there are a few useful idiomatic expressions using the verb *essere*.

essere al verde EHS-seh-ray ahl vehr-day	to be broke
essere in gioco EHS-seh-ray een joh-koh	to be at stake
essere nelle nuvole EHS-seh-ray nehl-leh NOO-voh-leh	to daydream, to have one's head in the clouds
essere un po' di fuori EHS-seh-ray oon poh dee foo-OHR-ee	to be out of one's mind

-SSENTIAL

There are numerous idiomatic expressions that use the verbs *fare, stare,* and *avere.* Try to master these verbs—it's the first step in learning how they are used idiomatically.

Idiomatic Expressions with *Stare*

The verb *stare* can mean "to feel," "to be," or "to stay," depending on the context. The following are its conjugations in the present tense:

stare (to stay, to feel), irregular *–are* verb

present
io sto
tu stai
lui, lei, Lei sta
noi stiamo
voi state
loro, Loro stanno

stare attento stah-ray ah-TEHN-toh	to pay attention
stare bene/male stah-ray beh-nay/mah-lay	to be well/not well
stare zitto stah-ray zee-toh	to keep quiet
stare fuori stah-ray foo-OHR-ee	to be outside
starsene da parte stahr-seh-neh da par-tay	to stand aside, to be on one side
stare su stah-ray soo	to stand (sit) up straight
stare a cuore stah-ray ah koo-OH-ray	to matter, to have at heart
stare con stah-ray kohn	to be with

stare in piedi	to be standing
stah-ray een pee-EH-dee	
stare in guardia	to be on one's guard
stah-ray een GWAHR-dee-ah	

Idiomatic Expressions with *Fare*

There are numerous idiomatic expressions using the verb *fare* (to do). Try not to get into the habit of translating these expressions word for word!

fare (to do, to make), irregular *–are* verb

present

io faccio

tu fai

lui, lei, Lei fa

noi facciamo

voi fate

loro, Loro fanno

fare attenzione	to pay attention
fah-ray aht-tehnts-YOH-nay	
fare il bagno	to take a bath
fah-ray eel ban-yoh	
fare caldo	to be hot (weather)
fah-ray kahl-doh	
fare colazione	to have breakfast
fah-ray koh-lahts-YOH-nay	
fare la doccia	to take a shower
fah-ray lah doh-chah	
fare una domanda	to ask a question
fah-ray oo-nah doh-MAHN-dah	

fare un errore fah-ray oon eh-ROHR-ay	to make a mistake
fare una foto fah-ray oo-nah foh-toh	to take a picture
fare freddo fah-ray frehd-doh	to be cold (weather)
fare una gita fah-ray oo-nah jee-tah	to take a short trip
fare un giro fah-ray oon jee-roh	to go for a ride
fare il grande fah-ray eel grahn-day	to show off
fare la guerra fah-ray lah gwehr-rah	to wage war
fare impazzire fah-ray eem-pahts-SEE-ray	to drive someone crazy
fare una passeggiata fah-ray oo-nah pahs-seh-JAH-tah	to take a walk
fare una pausa fah-ray oo-nah pow-zah	to take a break
fare un regalo fah-ray oon reh-GAH-loh	to give a gift
fare la spesa fah-ray lah speh-zah	to go food shopping
fare le spese fah-ray leh speh-zeh	to go shopping
fare un viaggio fah-ray oon vee-AH-joh	to take a trip

Common Idiomatic Expressions

The following expressions apply to a great variety of situations and are commonly used and understood throughout the Italian peninsula. Most can be used in both formal and informal situations.

A chi lo dici! ah kee loh dee-chee	You don't say!
a tutti i costi a toot-tee ee kohs-tee	at any cost; no matter what
Affare fatto. ahf-fah-ray faht-toh	It's a deal.
Alla buon'ora! ahl-lah boo-ohn oh-rah	It's about time!
Altroché! ahl-troh keh	Of course; you can bet your life!
Bell'affare! behl ahf-FAH-ray	That's really good (ironic)!
Bella roba! behl-lah roh-bah	Very nice! (ironic)
Beato te! bay-AH-toh teh	Lucky you!
Che barba! keh bahr-bah	How boring!
Che macello! keh mah-CHEL-loh	What a mess!
Che noia! keh noy-ah	How boring!
Che roba! keh roh-bah	I can't believe it!

Che schifo! keh skee-foh	How disgusting!
Che ti passa per la testa? keh tee pahs-sah pehr lah tess-tah	What's the matter with you?
Ci mancherebbe altro! chee mahn-keh-REHB-beh ahl-troh	God forbid
Ci vuole altro! chee voo-oh-leh ahl-troh	It takes much more than that.
d'altro canto dahl-troh kahn-toh	on the other hand
da morire dah moh-REE-reh	a lot
davvero? dahv-VEH-roh	really?
fa presente che. . . fah preh-ZEHN-teh keh	bear in mind . . .
Fatti gli affari tuoi. faht-tee lyee ahf-FAH-ree too-oi	Mind your own business.
fra l'altro. . . frah lahl-troh	among other things . . .
in ogni modo een ohn-yee moh-doh	anyway; at any cost
in poche parole een poh-keh pah-ROH-leh	in a few words
lascia perdere lah-shah PEHR-deh-ray	forget it
lascia stare lah-shah stah-ray	forget it
Lasciami stare. lah-shah mee stah-ray	Leave me alone.
Ma va. mah vah	I don't believe you; that's impossible.

Manco per sogno!	Not even in your dreams!
mahn-koh pehr sohn-yoh	
Meglio così.	It's better this way.
mehl-yoh koh-zee	
Meglio di niente.	Better than nothing at all.
mehl-yoh dee nee-EHN-teh	
Meno male!	Luckily!
may-noh mah-lay	
Non ne posso più.	I can't take it anymore.
nohn neh poh-soh pyou	
oggi come oggi	nowadays
oh-jee koh-meh oh-jee	
Per carità!	God forbid!
pehr kah-ree-TAH	
per farla breve	to cut it short
pehr fahr-lah breh-veh	
Porca miseria!	Damn it!
pohr-kah mee-ZEH-ree-ah	
Roba da matti.	That's crazy.
roh-bah dah maht-tee	
Sei sicuro/a?	Are you sure?
say see-KOO-roh/rah	
senz'altro	certainly
sehn-ZAHL-troh	
Siamo alle solite.	Here we go again.
see-AH-moh ah-leh SOH-lee-teh	
Sul serio?	Really?
sool SEH-ree-oh	
tanto meglio	so much the better
tahn-toh mehl-yoh	
tanto peggio	so much the worse
tahn-toh pehj-joh	

tieni presente. . . tee-EH-nee preh-zehn-tay	keep in mind . . .
tutt'altro toot-AHL-troh	on the contrary
Vale la pena. vah-lay lah peh-nah	It's worth it.

-SSENTIAL

> Learning idiomatic expressions is not easy. Try renting an Italian movie or buying an Italian CD—you're sure to find some idiomatic gems buried within!

What Your Teacher Never Taught You

By no means exhaustive, nor rife with vulgarities, the following list contains some fun and colorful expressions to be used in a variety of situations:

accidenti ah-chee-DEHN-tee	a mild expletive, like darn or heck
alito puzzolente AH-lee-toh poots-oh-LEHN-tay	bad breath
amore a prima vista ah-MOHR-ay ah pree-mah VEE-stah	love at first sight
arrapare ahr-rah-PAH-ray	to become sexually excited

bel niente behl nee-EHN-teh	nothing, nada, zip
bischero BEE-skeh-roh	a stupid person (Tuscany)
casino kah-ZEE-no	can mean "a lot" or "a mess" (*Mi è piaciuto un casino.* I liked it a lot. *Che casino!* What a mess!)
chiudere il becco KYEW-deh-ray eel behk-koh	to shut up, to shut one's trap
fannullone fahn-nool-LOH-nay	a lazy bum
fregare freh-GAHR-ay	to cheat or swindle somebody
fuori di testa fwoh-ree dee tess-ta	to be out of one's mind
leccaculo or *leccapiedi* LEHK-kah-KOO-loh leh-kah-PYAY-dee	brownnoser
mollare qualcuno mohl-lah-ray kwahl-KOO-noh	to dump someone
morire dalla noia moh-REE-reh dahl-lah noy-ah	to die of boredom
parolaccia pah-roh-LAHCH-ah	dirty word
pigrone/a pee-groh-nay/pee-groh-nah	a lazy bum
portare male gli anni pohr-TAH-ray mah-lay lyee ahn-nee	to age badly
roba da matti roh-bah dah maht-tee	crazy stuff

preso in giro	to be made fun of, made a
PRAY-zoh een JEE-roh	fool of
scemo/a	a stupid person, a jerk
sheh-moh/sheh-mah	
schifo	disgust, grossness (widely
SKEE-foh	used in expressions like *Che schifo!* "Ew! Gross!")
scocciare	to irritate or annoy
SKOH-chahr-ay	
valere la pena	to be worthwhile
vah-LEHR-ay lah pay-nah	

-SSENTIAL

If you hear an expression you don't understand, make sure you ask for clarification, or write it down so you can look it up later. Italian is a very colorful language, so don't miss out!

Appendix A

Italian/English Dictionary

a	at, to, in		**aereo**	airplane
a carico del destinatario	reverse charges/ collect call		**aeroporto**	airport
			Affare fatto.	It's a deal.
a casa	at home		**affittare**	to rent
A chi lo dici!	You don't say!		**affrancare**	stamp (verb)
a tutti i costi	at any cost; no matter what		**affrancatura**	postage
			africano	African
abbottonare	to button up		**agente di cambio**	stockbroker
accanto a	next to; beside			
accendere	to turn on/switch on		**aglio**	garlic
			agnello	lamb
accompagnatore	accompanist		**agosto**	August
accostare	to pull over to the side of the road		**Aiuto!**	Help!
			Al ladro!	Thief!
acqua (minerale)	water		**al sangue**	rare
Addio.	Goodbye (for good).		**albergo**	hotel
			albicocca	apricot
addormentarsi	to fall asleep; to go to sleep		**alimentari**	grocery store
			alito puzzolente	bad breath

Alla buon'ora!	It's about time!
alla destra	to the right
alla sinistra	to the left
alla/di moda	fashionable, in fashion
allacciare la cintura di sicurezza	to buckle your seat belt
allergia	allergy
allergico	allergic
alpinismo	mountain climbing
alto	tall
altro	other
Altroché!	Of course; you can bet your life!
alzarsi	to get up, to rise
ambra	amber
americano	American
amministratore delegato	CEO
ammorbidente	fabric softener
amore a prima vista	love at first sight
analisi	examination
analisi del sangue	blood test
anca	hip
ancora	more
andare	to go
andare a letto	to go to bed
anello	ring
anestesia locale	local anesthesia
anestetico	anesthetic

annodare	to knot, to tie
annoiarsi	to get bored
antipasto	antipasto
antipatico	unpleasant
anulare	ring finger
aperitivo	aperitif
aperto	open
apparecchio	braces
appartamento	apartment
appendicite	appendicitis
applaudire	to applaud, to clap
applauso	applause
apprendista	apprentice
aprile	April
aprire	to open
aprire le tende	to open/draw the curtains
arancia	orange
arancione	orange (in color)
arbitro	referee
area di rigore	penalty area
argentato	silver plated
argenteo	silver (in color), silvery
argento	silver
aria	air
aria condizionata	air conditioning
armadietto	cupboard
armadio	cabinet
armadio	closet, wardrobe

armadio per pratiche	filing cabinet
arrabbiarsi	to get angry
arrapare	to become sexually excited
arricciare i capelli	to curl
Arrivederci!	Bye!
arrivi	arrivals
arte	art
arteria	artery
artrite	arthritis
ascella	armpit
ascensore	elevator
ascesso	abscess
asciugamano	towel
asciugare	to dry
asciugare con il phon	to blow dry
ascoltare	to listen (to)
ascoltare la musica	to listen to music
asciugatrice	dryer
asmatico	asthmatic
asparagi	asparagus
aspirapolvere	vacuum cleaner
aspirina	aspirin
assegno	check
assistente	clerical assistant
assistente di bordo	steward/ stewardess
assonnato	tired
assumere	to hire

attentato	attack
Attenzione!	Watch out!
atterrare	to land
atto	act
attraente	attractive
attraversare	to cross
aula	classroom
aumento di stipendio	raise
Australia	Australia
australiano	Australian
autista	driver
automobile/auto	car
autobus	bus
automatico	automatic
autostrada	highway
autunno	autumn
avaro	greedy
avere	to have
avere + number + anni	to be _____ years old
avere bisogno di	to need, have need of
avere bisogno di medicina	to need medicine
avere caldo	to be warm (hot)
avere fame	to be hungry
avere freddo	to be cold
avere fretta	to be in a hurry
avere l'ipertensione	to have high blood pressure
avere l'ipotensione	to have low blood pressure

avere paura (di)	to be afraid (of)
avere ragione	to be right, correct
avere sete	to be thirsty
avere sonno	to be sleepy
avere torto	to be wrong, incorrect
avere un chiodo fisso in testa	to be fixated on something
avere voglia di	to want, to feel like
avvocato	lawyer
azalea	azalea
azienda	company
azzurro	blue (pale)
baffi	moustache
bagagli	baggage
bagagli da stiva	checked luggage
bagagliaio	trunk
bagaglio a mano	carry-on luggage
bagagli smarriti	lost luggage
bagno	bathroom
balcone	balcony
ballare	to dance
ballerino	dancer
balletto	ballet
ballo	dancing
bambino, bambina	child
banana	banana
banca	bank
banchiere	banker

banco di check-in	check-in desk
bancomat	ATM
banconota	banknote
bandierina d'angolo	corner flag
bar	coffee shop
barare	to cheat
barattola	jar
barba	beard
barbiere	barber
barista	bartender
barometro	barometer
baseball	baseball
basso	short
basta	enough
batteria	drums
Beato te!	Lucky you!
begonia	begonia
bel niente	nothing, nada, zip
belgo	Belgian
Bella roba!	Very nice! (ironic)
Bell'affare!	That's really good! (ironic)
bello	beautiful
ben cotto	well done
benda elastica	ace bandage
Bene, grazie.	Fine, thanks.
benzina	gas
bere	to drink

finestrino	window
fioraio	florist
firmare	to sign
flauto	flute
fodera	lining
foglie	leaves
foglio di carta	piece of paper
fontana	fountain
football americano	American football
footing	jogging
forchetta	fork
forfora	dandruff
formaggio	cheese
fornaio	bakery
fornello	burner (stove)
forno	oven
forno a microonde	microwave (oven)
foschia	mist
fotografia	photography
fra	between
fra l'altro	among other things
fragola	strawberry
francese	French
Francia	France
francobollo	stamp (noun)
francobollo emissione speciale	commemorative stamp
frangetta	strand

fratello	brother
freddo	cold
fregare	to cheat or swindle somebody
frigorifero	fridge
frizione	scalp massage
fronte	forehead
frutte	fruit
frutti di mare	seafood
fruttivendolo	green grocer
fucsia	fuchsia
fumatori	smokers
fuori	outside, outdoors
fuori di testa	to be out of one's mind
fuorigioco	offside
furto	burglary
gamba	leg
gara	competition, race
garage	garage
gardenia	gardenia
garofano	carnation
garza	gauze bandage
gelateria	ice cream shop
gelato	ice cream
gelato al cioccolato	chocolate ice cream
gelato alla fragola	strawberry ice cream
gelato alla vaniglia	vanilla ice cream

gelo	frost	giudice	judge
gelsomino	jasmine	giugno	June
gemelli da camicia	cufflinks	gladiolo	gladiolus
		glicine	wisteria
generoso	generous	globo oculare	eyeball
gengive	gums	gocce	drops
genitori	parents	golf	golf
gennaio	January	gomito	elbow
geranio	geranium	gomma	eraser
gesso	chalk	gomma	tire
ghiaccio	ice	gonna	skirt
giacca	jacket	gramma	gram
giacinto	hyacinth	grande	large; great
giallo	yellow	grande magazzino	department store
Giappone	Japan		
giapponese	Japanese	grandine	hail
giardini	gardens	grasso	fat
giardino	yard, garden	grazie	thank you
giglio	lily	grigio	gray
ginnastica	gymnastics	guancia	cheek
ginocchio	knee	guanti	gloves
giocatore	player	guardalinee	linesman
gioco dei birilli	bowling	guardaroba	coat check room
gioielleria	jewelry shop	guida telefonica	telephone directory
gioielli	jewelry		
giornalista	journalist	guidare	to drive
giovane	young	hotel	hotel
giovedì	Thursday	ibisco	hibiscus
gira a destra	turn right	icona	icon
gira a sinistra	turn left	imbarcare	to board
girare	to turn	immigrazione	immigration
		impermeabile	raincoat

impiegato	employee	**iniezione**	injection
impiegato dello stato	civil servant	**innamorarsi**	to fall in love
impiegato postale	postal clerk	**insalata**	salad
		insalatiera	salad bowl
imposta	shutter	**insetticida**	insect repellant
improvvisare	to improvise	**insonnia**	insomnia
in	in	**intelligente**	intelligent
in anticipo	early	**interruttore**	electrical switch
in linea	online	**intervallo**	intermission
in ogni modo	any way; or at any cost	**intervento**	operation
		intervista	interview
in poche parole	in a few words	**inverno**	winter
in ritardo	late	**investigatore**	detective
inamidato	starch(ed)	**ipercollegamento**	hyperlink
incassare un assegno	to cash (a check)	**ipertensione**	hypertension
		ippica	horse racing
incendio	fire	**iride**	iris
incidente	accident	**irlandese**	Irish
incinta	pregnant	**italiano**	Italian
incisivo	incisor	**jazz**	jazz
indiano	Indian	**jeans**	jeans
indice	index finger	**kilo**	kilogram
indirizzo	address	**labbro**	lip
infermiera	nurse	**laccio**	shoelace
infermiera di notte	night nurse	**lampada**	lamp
		lampadario	chandelier
informazione	information	**lampo**	lightning
infuso	infusion	**lampone**	raspberry
ingegnere	engineer	**lana**	wool
Inghilterra	England	**laringe**	larynx
inglese	English	**lascia perdere**	forget it

lasciami stare	leave me alone		**letteratura**	literature
lasciare un messaggio	to leave a message		**letto**	bed
lassativo	laxative		**letto matrimoniale**	double bed
latte	milk		**lettore DVD**	DVD player
latteria	dairy		**lettuga**	lettuce
latticini	dairy products		**libero**	sweeper
lattina	can		**libreria**	book shop
laurea	diploma (university)		**libro**	book
			licenziare	to fire
lavagna	chalkboard		**liceo**	high school
lavanderia a secco	dry cleaner		**lilla**	lilac
			limite di velocità	speed limit
lavandino	sink			
lavare	to wash		**limone**	lemon
lavare a secco	to dry clean		**linea di fondo**	goal line
lavarsi	to wash (oneself), to wash up		**linea di metà campo**	halfway line
lavarsi i denti	to clean/brush one's teeth		**linea laterale**	touch line
			lingua	tongue
lavastoviglie	dishwasher		**litro**	liter
lavatrice	washing machine		**lontano da**	far (from)
			luglio	July
lavorare	to work		**Lui si chiama . . .**	His name is . . .
lavoro	job			
leccaculo/ leccapiedi	brownnoser		**lunedì**	Monday
			lungo	long
leggere	to read		**Ma va.**	I don't believe you. That's impossible.
Lei si chiama . . .	Her name is . . .			
lenzuola	sheets		**macchia**	stain
lepre	hare		**macchina/ automobile/auto**	car
lettera	letter			

macchina grande	full-size car
macchina media	mid-size car
macchina piccola	economy car
macedonia di frutta	fruit salad
macelleria	butcher shop
madre (mamma)	mother
maggio	May
maglia	shirt (jersey)
maglietta	T-shirt
maglione	sweater
magnolia	magnolia
maiale	pork
mal di denti	toothache
mal di mare	seasickness
malato	sick
mancia	tip
Manco per sogno!	Not even in your dreams!
mangiare	to eat
manica	sleeve
mano	hand
manzo	beef
margherita	daisy
marito	husband
marocchino	Moroccan
marrone	brown
martedì	Tuesday
marzo	March
mascella	jaw
matrigna	stepmother
mattita	pencil
mediatore	broker
medicina	medicine
medio	medium
medio	middle finger
Meglio così.	It's better this way.
Meglio di niente.	Better than nothing at all.
mela	apple
melanzana	eggplant
meno	less, fewer
Meno male!	Luckily!
mento	chin
menù	menu
mercato	open-air market
mercato centrale	central market
mercoledì	Wednesday
merendina	snack
messa in scena	production
messicano	Mexican
metropolitana	subway
Mi chiamo . . .	My name is . . .
mi dispiace	I'm sorry
mi scusi	pardon me
mignolo	pinkie
mille grazie	thank you very much
mimosa	mimosa

minestra, minestrone	soup	mutande	underwear
mirtillo	blueberry	mutandine	panties
misura	clothing size	nascondino	hide and seek
misurare	to measure	naso	nose
mittente	sender	navigatore	browser
mobili	furniture	nebbia	fog
modello in gesso	plaster cast	negozio	store
modulo dogana	customs declaration form	negozio di giocattoli	toy store
moglie	wife	neozelandese	New Zealander
molare	molar	nero	black
mollare qualcuno	to dump someone	nervo	nerve
moneta	coin	neve	snow
monumento	monument	Nevica.	It's snowing.
moquette	carpet	niente da dichiarare	nothing to declare
mora	blackberry	nipote	nephew
morbido	soft, smooth	nipote	niece
morire dalla noia	to die of boredom	nipoti	grandchildren
mostra d'arte	art exhibit	no	no
moto	motorcycle	noioso	boring
motore di ricerca	search engine	nome	first name
		non affrancato	unstamped
motorino	moped	Non c'è di che.	You're welcome.
multimediale	multimedia	non fumatori	nonsmokers
muscolo	muscle	Non ne posso più.	I can't take it anymore.
museo	museum	nonna	grandmother
musica classica	classical music	nonni	grandparents
musica rock	rock music	nonno	grandfather
		nord	north
		notaio	notary

notte	one night
novembre	November
nudo	naked, bare, nude
numero di telefono	phone number
nuoto	swimming
nuovo	new
nuvola	cloud
nuvoloso	cloudy
o	or
oboe	oboe
occhiali	glasses
occhiali da sole	sunglasses
occupato	busy
odontoiatra	oral surgeon
offerta famiglia	family offer
offerta speciale	special offer
oggi come oggi	nowadays
olandese	Dutch
oltre	besides
ombrello	umbrella
opera	opera
operare	to operate
ora di punta	rush hour
orario delle visite	visiting hours
orario di apertura	opening hours
orchestra	orchestra
ordinare	to order
orecchini	earrings
orecchio	ear
oro	gold
orologio	clock, watch
ortensia	hydrangea
orto	vegetable garden
ortodontista	orthodontist
ospedale	hospital
osso	bone
osteria	inn
ostruzione	obstruction
Ottimo!	Excellent!
ottobre	October
otturare	fill
otturazione	filling
otturazione provvisoria	temporary filling
ovest	west
pacchetto	small parcel
pacco	package
padella	frying pan
padre (papà)	father
pagina	page
pala	shovel
palato	palate
palcoscenico	stage
pallacanestro	basketball
pallamano	handball
pallanuoto	water polo
pallavolo	volleyball
pallone	ball
palo	post

palpebra	eyelid
panetteria	bakery
panna montata	whipped cream
pannello di controllo	control panel
pantaloni	pants
pantofole	slippers
parabrezza	windshield
parcheggiare	to park
parcheggio	parking lot
parco	park
pareggio	tie score
parete	wall
parete divisoria	partition wall
Parla . . . ?	Do you speak . . . ? (formal)
parlare	to speak
Parli . . . ?	Do you speak . . . ? (informal)
parola d'accesso	password
parolaccia	dirty word
parole chiavi	keywords
parrucca	wig
parrucheria	beauty parlor
parruchiere	hairstylist
parte	part
partenza	departure
partenze	departures
partire	to leave
partita	game
parucchiere/ barbiere	hairdresser/ barber

passaggio	pass
passaggio corto	short pass
passaporto	passport
passatempo	pastime
passeggero	passenger
pasticceria	pastry shop
pastiglia	pill
pasto	meal
patinaggio	skating
patrigno	stepfather
pavimento	floor
paziente	patient
pedonale	pedestrian
pelle	skin
penicillina	penicillin
penna	pen
pennarello	felt-tip pen
pennello	paintbrush
pentola	saucepan
per	for
Per carità!	God forbid!
per farla breve	to cut it short
per favore/per piacere/per cortesia	please
pera	pear
perché	why
perdere	to lose
perdere un dente	to lose a tooth
perforatore	punch
perle	pearls

persona	person
pesca	peach
pesce	fish
pescheria	fish market, fishmonger
pettinare	to comb
pettinarsi	to comb one's hair
pettinatura	hairstyle
pettine	comb
petunia	petunia
phon	hairdryer
Piacere mio.	It's my pleasure.
pian terreno	first floor (U.S.), ground floor (Italy)
piano	floor, story
pianoforte	piano
piatto	plate
piatto fondo	soup bowl
piccolo	small
piede	foot
pigiama	pajamas
pigro	lazy
pigrone/a	lazy bum
pilota	pilot
pioggia	rain
Piove.	It's raining.
piovere	to rain
piscina	pool
piselli	peas
pittura	painting

più grande	larger
più piccolo	smaller
più tardi	later
pizzaiolo	pizza maker
pizzeria	pizzeria
pneumatico	tire
poesia	poetry
polacco	Polish
Polizia!	Police!
polizotto	police officer
pollice	thumb
pollo	chicken
polmonite	pneumonia
polpaccio	calf
polso	wrist
poltrona	armchair
polvere	dust
pompelmo	grapefruit
ponte	bridge
popolare	popular
Porca miseria!	Damn it!
porta	door
portafoglio	wallet
portare male gli anni	to age badly
portiere	goalkeeper
portoghese	Portuguese
posate	silverware
posta aerea	air mail
postino	postman
posto	seat

povero	poor
pranzo	lunch
prato	lawn
preferire	to prefer
Prego.	You're welcome.
Prego.	Please./Here you are.
preludio	overture
prendere una multa	to get a ticket
prenotazione	reservation
prepararsi	to get ready
presa (di corrente)	electric socket
preservativi	prophylactics
presidente	president
preso in giro	to be made fun of, made a fool of
prima	before
prima classe	first class
primavera	spring
primo (piatto)	first course
primo piano	second floor (U.S.), first floor (Italy)
produttore	producer
profumeria	perfume store
profumo	perfume
programma	program
programmazione aziendale	corporate planning
prosciutto	ham

protesi	false tooth
prova generale	dress rehearsal
provare	to try
pugilato	boxing
pulire	to clean
pulito	clean
Può dirmi . . . ?	Can you tell me . . . ? (formal)
Puoi dirmi . . . ?	Can you tell me . . . ? (informal)
quaderno	notebook
quadro ematologico	blood count
quando	when
questo pomeriggio	this afternoon
raccoglitore delle schede	suspension file
raccomandata	register letter
radice	root
radio	radio
raffreddato	sick with a cold
raffreddore	cold
rallentare	to slow down
rammendare	to mend, to repair; to darn
rappresentazione	performance
rastrello	rake
ravanello	radish
receptionist	receptionist
recinto	fence
recitare	to act

reggiseno	bra
reparto di cure intensive	intensive care unit
rete	Internet
retina or portabagagli	luggage rack (overhead)
riagganciare	to hang up
riattaccare	to hang up
riavviare	to restart
riccioli	curls
ricco	rich
ricercatore	researcher
ricetta	prescription
ricevuta	receipt
richiamare	to call back
ridotto	lobby
rifare il booting	to reboot
riga	part
riga	ruler
rimedio	remedy
rimessa laterale	throw-in
riparare	to repair
ripetere	to repeat
riposarsi	to relax
riscaldamento centrale	central heating
ristorante	restaurant
ritiro bagagli	baggage claim
riunione	meeting
roba da matti	crazy stuff
romanzo	novel
rompersi il braccio/la gamba	to break one's arm/leg
rosa	pink
rosa	rose
rossetto	lipstick
rosso	red
rovesciata	bicycle kick
rozzo	rough, coarse
rubino	ruby
russo	Russian
sabato	Saturday
sala da pranzo	dining room
salario	salary
saldi	sale
salsiccia	sausage
salumeria	delicatessen
Salve!	Hello! (formal)
sandali	sandals
sanguinare	to bleed
sapone	soap
sassofono	saxophone
sbottonare	to unbutton, to undo
scacchi	chess
scaffale	shelf; bookcase
scala	staircase, stairs
scanner	scanner
scaricare	to download
scarpe	shoes
scarpe da ginnastica	sneakers

scattola	box
scemo/a	stupid person, a jerk
scenario	scenery
schifo	disgust, grossness
sci di discesa	downhill skiing
sci di fondo	cross-country skiing
sci nautico	waterskiing
sciacquare	to rinse
sciarpa	scarf
scienzato	scientist
sciroppo per la tosse	cough syrup
scocciare	to irritate or annoy
scolapiatti	drying rack
scompartimento	cabin
sconfitta	defeat
scopa	broom
scozzese	Scottish
scrittore	writer
scrivania	desk
scultura	sculpture
scuola	school
scuola media	junior high school
sdraiarsi	to lie down
secchio	bucket
secco	dry
seconda classe	second class
secondo (piatto)	second course

sedano	celery
sedersi	to sit down
sedersi	to sit down
sedia	chair
segnale acustico	dial tone
segretaria	secretary
segreteria telefonica	answering machine
Sei sicuro/a?	Are you sure?
semaforo	traffic lights
sempre diritto	straight ahead
senso unico	one way
sentirsi	to feel
senza	without
senz'altro	certainly
separato	separated
serratura	lock
servizio	service charge
servizio sveglia	wake-up call
seta	silk
settembre	September
setticemia	blood poisoning
settimana prossima	next week
sgabello	stool
shampoo	shampoo
shuttle	shuttle
sì	yes
siamo alle solite	here we go again
signora	ma'am, Mrs.
signore	sir, Mr.
signorina	miss

simpatico	kind	**spazzolare**	to brush
sinistra	left	**spazzolarsi i denti**	to brush (one's teeth)
sipario	curtain		
sistema operativo	operating system	**specchietto**	rearview mirror
		specchio	mirror
sito	site	**spesso**	thick
smeraldo	emerald	**spettacolo**	show
snello	slender	**spettatori**	spectators
soffitta	attic	**spilla**	brooch
soffitto	ceiling	**spillatrice**	stapler
soggiorno	living room	**spillo**	pin
soldato	soldier	**spina dorsale**	spine
sole	sun	**spinaci**	spinach
Sono . . .	I am . . .	**spogliarsi**	to undress (oneself), to get undressed
Sono di . . .	I am from . . .		
sopra	above		
sopracciglio	eyebrow	**sporco**	dirty
sorbetto ai lamponi	raspberry sherbet	**sport**	sport
		sportello	counter
sorbetto al limone	lemon sherbet	**sposarsi**	to get married
		sposato	married
sorbetto al arancia	orange sherbet	**spuntatina**	trim
		squadra	team
sorella	sister	**squillare**	to ring
sorpassare	to pass/overtake	**stampante**	printer
sotto	under	**stampe**	printed matter
Spagna	Spain	**stanza**	room
spagnolo	Spanish	**stare a cuore**	to matter, to have at heart
spalla	shoulder		
spazzatura	garbage	**stare attento**	to pay attention
spazzola	brush	**stare bene (a)**	to fit; to suit
spazzola per i denti	toothbrush	**stare bene/male**	to be well/unwell

stare con	to be with
stare fuori	to be outside
stare in guardia	to be on one's guard
stare in piedi	to be standing
stare su	to stand (sit) up straight
stare zitto	to keep quiet
starnutire	to sneeze
starsene da parte	to stand aside, to be on one side
stasera	this evening
Stati Uniti	United States
stazione	train station
stazione dei taxi	taxi stand
stendere il bucato	to hang up the wash/laundry
sterlina	British pound sterling
stesso	same
Stia in linea.	Please hold.
stirare	to iron
stitichezza	constipated
stivali	boots
stomaco	stomach
stop	stop
straccio	cloth, rag
strada senza uscita	dead end
strappo muscolare	sprain
stretto	tight(-fitting)

strisce pedonali	pedestrian crosswalk
strumento	instrument
studio	study
stupido	stupid
su	on
sud	south
Sul serio?	Really?
suocera	mother-in-law
suocero	father-in-law
suonare	to ring
suonare a orecchio	to play by ear
suonare a prima vista	to play by sight
suonare il pianoforte	to play the piano
suonare la chitarra	to play the guitar
supermercato	supermarket
svedese	Swedish
sveglia	alarm clock
svegliarsi	to wake up
svenire	to faint
svizzero	Swiss
tabaccaio	tobacco shop
tacchino	turkey
tacco a spillo	spike heel
taglia	clothing size
tagliaerba	lawnmower
tagliare	to cut
taglio di capelli	haircut
tangenziale	bypass road

tanto meglio	so much the better
tanto peggio	so much the worse
tappeto	rug, mat
tartaro	tartar
tasca	pocket
tasso di cambio	exchange rate
tastiera	keyboard
tavo la calda	buffet-style restaurant
tavola	table
taxi	taxi
tazza	cup
tè	cup of tea
teatro	theater
tecnico	technician
tedesco	German
telefonare	to call
telefonata	telephone call
telefonino/cellulare	cell phone
telefono	telephone
telegramma	telegram
televisore	television set
temperamatite	pencil sharpener
tempesta	storm
tempia	temple
tempo libero	free time
temporale	rainstorm
tenda	curtain
tenda da doccia	shower curtain

tennis	tennis
tergicristalli	windshield wipers
terminal	terminal
termometro	thermometer
termosifone	radiator
tessuto	cloth, fabric, material
testa	head
tetto	roof
tieni presente	keep in mind
tifoso	fan
timbrare	validate
tingere	to dye/to color
Tira vento.	It's windy.
titolo	title
togliere	to take off, to remove
toilette	toilet
tonsille	tonsils
torace	chest
tormenta	blizzard
torta	cake
torta di frutta	fruit tart
tosse	cough
tossire	to cough
tostapane	toaster
tovaglia	tablecloth
tovagliolo	napkin
tra	between
trachea	throat
tragedia	tragedy

tranne	except
tranquillante	tranquilizer
trasfusione di sangue	blood transfusion
trattamento della radice	root canal work
trattoria	restaurant (small)
travelers check	traveler's check
traversa	crossbar
treno	train
triste	sad
tromba	trumpet
trombone	trombone
troppo	too much, too many
trucco	makeup
tulipano	tulip
tutt'altro	on the contrary
tutte le direzioni	all routes/ directions
ulcera	ulcer
umido	damp, moist
un po' di	a little
unghia	nail
università	university
uscita	exit
uscita	gate (airport)
uva	grape
vagone letto	sleeper car
vai diritto	go straight
Vale la pena.	It's worth it.

valere la pena	to be worth the trouble
valuta	currency
variabile	changeable
varicella	chicken pox
vasca da bagno	bathtub
vaselina	vaseline
vaso	vase
vecchio	old
vedere	to see
vedovo	widowed
velluto	velvet
vena	vein
venerdì	Friday
Vengo da . . .	I come from . . .
verde	green
verniciare	to paint; to varnish
vero	true
verso	toward
vestirsi	to dress (oneself), to get dressed
vestiti	clothes
vestito da donna	dress
viaggia	to travel
vicino a	near
videoregistratore	VCR
vietata la sosta	no stopping
vietato parcheggiare	no parking
vincere	to win
vino	wine

viola	purple, violet	**yogurt**	yogurt
violentare	to rape	**zaffiro**	sapphire
violino	violin	**zaino**	backpack
violoncello	cello	**zappa**	hoe
visitare	to examine	**zia**	aunt
viso	face	**zinnia**	zinnia
visto	visa	**zio**	uncle
vitello	veal	**zucchero**	sugar
vittoria	victory	**zuppa**	soup
volante	steering wheel		
volo	flight		
vomitare	to vomit		

Appendix B

English/Italian Dictionary

a little	un po' di
a lot	da morire
able	bravo
above	sopra
abscess	ascesso
accident	incidente
accompanist	accompagnatore
accountant	contabile
ace bandage	benda elastica
act	atto
address	indirizzo
addressee	destinatario
adhesive bandage	cerotto
African	africano
after-dinner drink	digestivo
air	aria

air conditioning	aria condizionata, climatizzatore
air mail	posta aerea
airline	compagnia aerea
airplane	aereo
airport	aeroporto
alarm clock	sveglia
all routes/ directions	tutte le direzioni
allergic	allergico
allergy	allergia
amber	ambra
ambulance	un'ambulanza
American	americano
American football	football americano
among other things	fra l'altro

and	e
anesthetic	anestetico
ankle	caviglia
answering machine	segreteria telefonica
antipasto	antipasto
any way or at any cost	in ogni modo
apartment	appartamento
aperitif	aperitivo
appendicitis	appendicite
applause	applauso
apple	mela
apprentice	apprendista
apricot	albicocca
April	aprile
Are you sure?	Sei sicuro/a?
arm	braccio
armchair	poltrona
armpit	ascella
arrivals	arrivi
art	arte
art exhibit	mostra d'arte
artery	arteria
arthritis	artrite
artichoke	carciofo
asparagus	asparagi
aspirin	aspirina
asthmatic	asmatico
at any cost; no matter what	a tutti i costi
at	a
at home	a casa
at the dentist's office	dal dentista
ATM	bancomat
attack	attentato
attic	soffitta
attractive	attraente
August	agosto
aunt	zia
Australia	Australia
Australian	australiano
auto racing	corsa automobilistica
automatic	automatico
autumn	autunno
azalea	azalea
baby	bimbo, bimba
backpack	zaino
bad	cattivo
bad breath	alito puzzolente
baggage	bagagli
baggage check	consegna bagagli
baggage claim	ritiro bagagli
bakery	fornaio
bakery	panetteria
balcony	balcone
ball	pallone
ballet	balletto
banana	banana
bank	banca
bank teller	cassiere

banker	banchiere	**bicycle kick**	rovesciata
banknote	banconota	**bicycling**	ciclismo
barber	barbiere	**bill**	conto
barometer	barometro	**biologist**	biologo
bartender	barista	**bit, piece**	un po' di
baseball	baseball	**black**	nero
basketball	pallacanestro	**blackberry**	mora
bath; bathroom	bagno	**blanket**	coperta
bathing suit	costume da bagno	**bleach**	candeggina
bathroom	bagno	**blizzard**	tormenta
bathtub	vasca da bagno	**blonde**	biondo
beans	fagioli	**blood count**	quadro ematologico
bear in mind	fa presente che	**blood poisoning**	setticemia
beard	barba		
beautiful	bello	**blood test**	analisi del sangue
beauty parlor	parrucheria	**blood transfusion**	trasfusione di sangue
bed	letto		
bedroom	camera da letto	**blotter**	carteli da scrittoio
beef	manzo		
beer	birra	**blouse**	camicetta
before	prima	**blue (dark)**	blu
begonia	begonia	**blue (pale)**	azzurro
behind	dietro	**blueberry**	mirtillo
Belgian	belgo	**boarding pass**	carta d'imbarco
belt	cintura	**boat racing**	corsa nautica
beside	accanto a	**bocce ball**	bocce
besides	oltre	**body**	corpo
better than nothing at all	meglio di niente	**bone**	osso
		book	libro
between	tra, fra	**book shop**	libreria
bicycle	bicicletta	**bookcase**	scaffale

boots	stivali
boring	noioso
boss, manager	dirigente
brother-in-law	cognato
bottle	bottiglia
bowl	ciotola
bowling	gioco dei birilli
box	scattola
boxing	pugilato
bra	reggiseno
bracelet	braccialetto
braces	apparecchio
brain	cervello
Brazilian	brasiliano
breakfast	colazione
bridge	ponte
British pound sterling	sterlina
broker	mediatore
brooch	spilla
broom	scopa
brother	fratello
brown	marrone
browser	navigatore
brush	spazzola
bucket	secchio
buffet	credenza
buffet-style restaurant	tavola calda
burglary	furto
burner (stove)	fornello
bus	autobus
bus stop	fermata dell'autobus
business card	carta da visita
busy	occupato
butcher shop	macelleria
butter	burro
button	bottone
by	da
bypass road	tangenziale
cabbage	cavolo
cabin	scompartimento
cabinet	armadio
cake	torta
calf	polpaccio
camping	campeggio
can	lattina
Can you tell me . . . ? (formal)	Può dirmi . . . ?
Can you tell me . . . ? (informal)	Puoi dirmi . . . ?
Canada	Canada
Canadian	canadese
car	carrozza
car	macchina/ automobile/auto
car hood	cofano
cards	carte
carnation	garofano
carpet	moquette
carrot	carotta
carry-on luggage	bagaglio a mano
cart	carello

cash register	cassa	**chest**	torace
cashier	cassiera	**chest of drawers**	cassettone
cathedral	cattedrale		
cavities	carie	**chicken**	pollo
ceiling	soffitto	**chicken pox**	varicella
celery	sedano	**chief conductor**	capotreno
cell phone	telefonino/ cellulare	**child**	bambino, bambina
cello	violoncello	**chimney**	camino
central heating	riscaldamento centrale	**chin**	mento
		China	Cina
central market	mercato centrale	**Chinese**	cinese
		chocolate	cioccolato
CEO	amministratore delegato	**chocolate ice cream**	gelato al cioccolato
certainly	senz'altro	**chorus**	coro
chair	sedia	**chrysanthemum**	crisantemo
chalk	gesso	**church**	chiesa
chalkboard	lavagna	**cinema**	cinema
championship	campionato	**civil servant**	impiegato dello stato
chandelier	lampadario		
change	cambio	**clarinet**	clarinetto
changeable	variabile	**classical music**	musica classica
check	assegno	**classroom**	aula
check/bill	conto	**clean**	pulito
checked luggage	bagagli da stiva	**clerical assistant**	assistente
check-in desk	banco di check-in	**climate**	clima
		clock	orologio
cheek	guancia	**closed**	chiuso
cheese	formaggio	**closet**	armadio
cherry	ciliegia	**cloth**	tessuto
chess	scacchi	**cloth**	straccio

clothes	vestiti	constipated	stitichezza
clothing size	taglia, misura	contract	contratto
cloud	nuvola	control panel	pannello di controllo
cloudy	nuvoloso		
coat check room	guardaroba	convertible	decapotabile
		cook	cuoco/chef
coffee	caffè	cookie	biscotto
coffee shop	bar	corner flag	bandierina d'angolo
coffeemaker	caffettiera		
coin	moneta	corporate planning	programmazione aziendale
coin changer	distributore monete		
		corridor	corridoio
cold (temperature)	freddo	costume jewelry	bigiotteria
cold (illness)	raffreddore	costumes	costumi
cold (sick with a)	raffreddato	cotton	cotone
collarbone	clavicola	couch, sofa	divano
collect call	a carico del destinario	cough	tosse
		cough syrup	sciroppo per la tosse
color	colore		
comb	pettine	counter	sportello
comedy	commedia	course	corso
comfortable	comodo	cousin	cugino, cugina
commemorative stamp	francobollo emissione speciale	cover charge	coperto
		crazy stuff	roba da matti
		crossbar	traversa
company	azienda	cross-country skiing	sci di fondo
competition	gara		
computer	computer	crossword puzzle	cruciverba
concert	concerto		
conductor	controllore	crown	corona
conductor	direttore d'orchestra	cufflinks	gemelli da camicia

cup	tazza	**delicatessen**	salumeria
cup of coffee	caffè	**dental clinic**	clinica odontoiatrica
cup of tea	tè	**dentist**	dentista
cupboard	armadietto	**denture**	dentiera
curls	riccioli	**department store**	grande magazzino
currency	valuta	**departure**	partenza
curtain	tenda	**departures**	partenze
curtain	sipario	**desk**	scrivania
cuspid	canino	**desk drawer**	cassetto della scrivania
customs	dogana	**dessert**	dessert/dolce
customs declaration	dichiarazione doganale	**destination**	destinazione
customs declaration form	modulo dogana	**detective**	investigatore
dahlia	dalia	**diabetes**	diabete
dairy	latteria	**diabetic**	diabetico
dairy products	latticini	**diagnosis**	diagnosi
daisy	margherita	**dial tone**	segnale acustico
Damn it!	Porca miseria!	**dialog box**	finestra di dialogo
damp, moist	umido	**diamond**	diamante
dancer	ballerino	**dictionary**	dizionario
dancing	ballo	**diesel**	diesel
dandruff	forfora	**digestive tonic**	digestivo
dark-haired	bruno	**dining room**	sala da pranzo
darts	dardi	**dinner**	cena
daughter	figlia	**dinner plate**	piatto
dead end	strada senza uscita	**diploma (high school)**	diploma
dear	caro	**diploma (university)**	laurea
December	dicembre	**dirty**	sporco
defeat	sconfitta		

dirty word	parolaccia	dry hair	capelli secchi
discharge	dimettere dall'ospedale	dryer	asciugatrice
		drying rack	scolapiatti
disgust	schifo	duet	duetto
dishwasher	lavastoviglie	dusk	crepuscolo
disinfectant	disinfettante	dust	polvere
divorced	divorziato(a)	Dutch	olandese
dizziness	capogiro	DVD player	lettore DVD
Do you speak . . . ? (formal)	Parla . . . ?	ear	orecchio
		early	in anticipo
Do you speak . . . ? (informal)	Parli . . . ?	earrings	orecchini
		east	est
doctor	dottore/ dottoressa	economist	economista
doctorate degree	dottorato	economy car	macchina piccola
dollar	dollaro	eggplant	melanzana
door	porta	Egyptian	egiziano
double bed	letto matrimoniale	elbow	gomito
		electric socket	presa (di corrente)
downhill skiing	sci di discesa		
drama	dramma	electric stove	cucina elettrica
drawer	cassetto	electrical switch	interruttore
drawing	disegno		
dress	vestito da donna	elegant	elegante
dress rehearsal	prova generale	elevator	ascensore
dribble	dribbling	emerald	smeraldo
driver	autista	employee	impiegato
drops	gocce	engineer	ingegnere
drums	batteria	England	Inghilterra
dry	secco	English	inglese
dry cleaner	lavanderia a secco	enough	basta
		entertaining	divertente

entertainment	divertimento	**field**	campo di calcio
entrance	entrata	**filing cabinet**	armadio per pratiche
eraser	gomma		
European	europeo	**fill**	otturare
examination	analisi	**filling**	otturazione
excellent	ottimo	**Fine, thanks.**	Bene, grazie.
except	tranne	**finger**	dito
exchange rate	tasso di cambio	**fire**	incendio
exit	uscita	**fireplace**	caminetto
eyeball	globo oculare	**first class**	prima classe
eyebrow	sopracciglio	**first course**	primo (piatto)
eyelid	palpebra	**first floor (U.S.), ground floor (Italy)**	pian terreno
fabric	tessuto		
fabric softener	ammorbidente	**first name**	nome
face	viso	**fish**	pesche
false tooth	protesi	**fish market, fishmonger**	pescheria
family offer	offerta famiglia		
fan	tifoso	**flight**	volo
far (from)	lontano da	**flood**	deluvione
fashionable, in fashion	alla/di moda	**floor**	pavimento
		floor, story	piano
fat	grasso	**florist**	fioraio
father	padre (papà)	**flute**	flauto
father-in-law	suocero	**fog**	nebbia
February	febbraio	**folder**	cartella
felt-tip pen	pennarello	**foot**	piede
fence	recinto	**footwear**	calzatura
fever	febbre	**for**	per
fewer	meno	**forehead**	fronte
fiancé	fidanzato	**Forget it.**	Lascia perdere. or Lascia stare.
fiancée	fidanzata		

fork	forchetta	**gas station**	distributore di benzina
foul	fallo	**gas stove**	cucina a gas
fountain	fontana	**gate**	cancello
France	Francia	**gate (airport)**	uscita
free kick	calcio di punizione	**gauze bandage**	garza
free time	tempo libero	**generous**	generoso
freezer	congelatore	**geranium**	geranio
French	francese	**German**	tedesco
Friday	venerdì	**gladiolus**	gladiolo
fridge	frigorifero	**glass**	bicchiere
from	da, di (d')	**glass of orange juice**	bicchiere di succo d'arancia
frost	gelo		
frostbite	congelamento	**glasses**	occhiali
fruit	frutte	**gloves**	guanti
fruit salad	macedonia di frutta	**go straight**	vai diritto
		goal kick	calcio di rinvio
fruit stand	fruttivendola	**goal line**	linea di fondo
fruit tart	torta di frutta	**goalkeeper**	portiere
frying pan	padella	**God forbid!**	Ci mancherebbe altro!
fuchsia	fucsia		
full-size car	macchina grande	**God forbid!**	Per carità!
		gold	oro
furniture	mobili	**gold (in color), golden**	d'orato
game	partita		
garage	garage	**gold plated**	dorato
garbage	spazzatura	**golden, made of gold**	d'oro
gardenia	gardenia		
gardens	giardini	**golf**	golf
garlic	aglio	**good**	buono
gas	benzina	**Goodbye.**	Arrive derci.
		Goodbye. (for good)	Addio.

Good day.	Buon giorno.
Good evening.	Buona sera.
Good morning.	Buona mattina.
Goodnight.	Buona notte.
good	bravo
gram	gramma
grandchildren	nipoti
grandfather	nonno
grandmother	nonna
grandparents	nonni
grape	uva
grapefruit	pompelmo
grass	erba
gray	grigio
great	grande
greedy	avaro
green	verde
green grocer	fruttivendolo
grocery store	alimentari
guitar	chitarra
gums	gengive
gunshot	colpo di pistolla
gymnastics	ginnastica
hail	grandine
hair	capelli
hairstyle	pettinatura
hairstylist	parruchiere
haircut	taglio di capelli
hairdresser/ barber	parucchiere/ barbiere
hairdryer	phon

halfway line	linea di metà campo
hallway	corridoio
ham	prosciutto
hand	mano
handbag	borsa
handball	pallamano
happy	felice
hardware store	ferramenta
hare	lepre
hat	cappello
head	testa
header	colpo di testa
heart	cuore
heartburn	bruciore di stomaco
hectogram	etto
heel	calcagno
Hello! (formal)	Salve!
help	aiuto
Her name is . . .	Lei si chiama . . .
Here we go again.	Siamo alle solite.
Hi! (informal)	Ciao!
hibiscus	ibisco
hide-and-seek	nascondino
high school	liceo
highway	autostrada
hiking	excursionismo
hip	anca
His name is . . .	Lui si chiama . . .
hoe	zappa

homework	compiti
horseback riding	equitazione
horse racing	ippica
hospital	ospedale
hot	caldo
hotel	hotel/albergo
house; home	casa
how	come
How are you?	Come stai?
How boring.	Che barba. or Che noia.
How disgusting!	Che schifo!
hunting	caccia
husband	marito
hyacinth	giacinto
hydrangea	ortensia
hyperlink	ipercollegamento
hypertension	ipertensione
I am . . .	Sono . . .
I am from . . .	Sono di . . .
I can't take it anymore.	Non ne posso più.
I can't believe it.	Che roba.
I come from . . .	Vengo da . . .
I don't believe you. That's impossible.	Ma va.
I'm sorry	mi dispiace
ice	ghiaccio
ice cream	gelato
ice cream shop	gelateria

icon	icona
immigration	immigrazione
in	in, a
in a few words	in poche parole
in back of	dietro
in cash	con contanti
in front	davanti
in front of	davanti a
inbox	casella di posta elettronica
incisor	incisivo
index finger	indice
Indian	indiano
information	informazione
infusion	infuso
injection	iniezione
inn	osteria
insect repellant	insetticida
inside, indoors	dentro
insomnia	insonnia
instrument	strumento
intelligent	intelligente
intensive care unit	reparto di cure intensive
intermission	intervallo
Internet	rete
interview	intervista
iris	iride
Irish	irlandese
iron	ferro da stiro
It's my pleasure.	Piacere mio.

It takes much more than that.	Ci vuole altro.	June	giugno
It's about time.	Alla buon'ora.	junior high school	scuola media
It's better this way.	Meglio così.	keep in mind	tieni presente
Italian	italiano	kettle	bollitore
It's a deal.	Affare fatto.	key	chiave
It's cold.	Fa freddo.	keyboard	tastiera
It's foggy.	C'è la nebbia.	keywords	parole chiavi
It's hot.	Fa caldo.	kilogram	kilo
It's nice.	Fa bel tempo.	kind	simpatico
It's raining.	Piove	kitchen	cucina
It's snowing.	Nevica.	knee	ginocchio
It's sunny.	C'è il sole.	knife	coltello
It's windy.	Tira vento.	lamb	agnello
It's worth it.	Vale la pena.	lamp	lampada
jacket	giacca	lane	corsia
January	gennaio	large	grande
Japan	Giappone	larger	più grande
Japanese	giapponese	larynx	laringe
jar	barattola	last name	cognome
jasmine	gelsomino	late	in ritardo
jaw	mascella	later	piu' tardi
jazz	jazz	lawn	prato
jeans	jeans	lawnmower	tagliaerba
jewelry	gioielli	lawyer	avvocato
jewelry shop	gioielleria	laxative	lassativo
job	lavoro	lazy	pigro
jogging	footing	lazy bum	fannullone
journalist	giornalista	lazy bum	pigrone/a
judge	giudice	leather	cuoio
July	luglio	Leave me alone.	Lasciami stare.
		leaves	foglie

left	sinistra
leg	gamba
lemon	limone
lemon sherbet	sorbetto al limone
less	meno
letter	lettera
lettuce	lettuga
lightning	lampo
lights	fari
lilac	lilla
lily	giglio
linesman	guardalinee
lining	fodera
lip	labbro
lipstick	rossetto
liter	litro
literature	letteratura
liver	fegato
living room	soggiorno
lobby	ridotto
local anesthesia	anestesia locale
lock	serratura
long	lungo
lost luggage	bagagli smarriti
love at first sight	amore a prima vista
luckily	meno male
Lucky you.	Beato te.
luggage rack (overhead)	retina or portabagagli
lunch	pranzo

ma'am, Mrs.	signora
magnolia	magnolia
mailbox	buca delle lettere
makeup	trucco
manager	dirigente/ manager
March	marzo
married	sposato
May	maggio
meal	pasto
meat	carne
medical director	direttore medico
medicine	medicina
medium	medio
meeting	riunione
menu	menù
mess	casino
Mexican	messicano
microwave (oven)	forno a microonde
middle finger	medio
midfield player	centrocampista
mid-size car	macchina media
milk	latte
mimosa	mimosa
Mind your own business.	Fatti gli affari tuoi.
mirror	specchio
miss	signorina
mist	foschia
molar	molare

Monday	lunedì
money	denaro/soldi
monument	monumento
moped	motorino
more	ancora
Moroccan	marocchino
mother	madre (mamma)
mother-in-law	suocera
motorcycle	moto
mountain climbing	alpinismo
moustache	baffi
mouth	bocca
multimedia	multimediale
muscle	muscolo
museum	museo
My luggage is lost.	I miei bagagli sono smarriti.
My name is . . .	Mi chiamo . . .
nail	unghia
naked	nudo
napkin	tovagliolo
near	vicino a
neck	collo
necklace	collana
nephew	nipote
nerve	nervo
new	nuovo
New Zealander	neozelandese
newsstand	edicola, giornalaio
next to	accanto a

next week	settimana prossima
niece	nipote
night nurse	infermiera di notte
no	no
no parking	vietato parcheggiare
no stopping	vietata la sosta
nonsmokers	non fumatori
north	nord
nose	naso
Not even in your dreams.	Manco per sogno.
notary	notaio
notebook	quaderno
nothing to declare	niente da dichiarare
nothing, nada, zip	bel niente
novel	romanzo
November	novembre
nowadays	oggi come oggi
nude	nudo
nurse	infermiera
oboe	oboe
obstruction	ostruzione
October	ottobre
of course; you can bet your life	altro ché
of	di (d')
offside	fuorigioco

oily hair	capelli grassi		outdoors	fuori
okay	d'accordo		oven	forno
old	vecchio		overcoat	cappotto
on	su		overture	preludio
on the contrary	tutt'altro		package	pacco
on the other hand	d'altro canto		page	pagina
			pain	dolore
one night	notte		paintbrush	pennello
one person	persona		painting	pittura
one way	senso unico		pajamas	pigiama
one-way ticket	biglietto solo andata		palate	palato
			panties	mutandine
onion	cipolla		pants	pantaloni
online	in linea		paper	carta
open	aperto		paper clip	fermaglio
open-air market	mercato		paper store	cartoleria
opening hours	orario di apertura		Pardon me.	Mi scusi.
			parents	genitori
opera	opera		park	parco
operating system	sistema operativo		parking lot	parcheggio
operation	intervento		part	parte
or	o		part	riga
oral surgeon	odontoiatra		partition wall	parete divisoria
orange	arancia		pass	passaggio
orange (color)	arancione		passenger	passeggero
orange sherbet	sorbetto al arancia		passport	passaporto
			password	parola d'accesso
orchestra	orchestra		pastime	passatempo
orthodontist	ortodontista		pastry shop	pasticceria
other	altro		patient	paziente
outdoor market	mercato		pay envelope	busta paga

peach	pesca	pink	rosa
pear	pera	pinkie	mignolo
pearls	perle	pizza maker	pizzaiolo
peas	piselli	pizzeria	pizzeria
pedestrian	pedonale	plaster cast	modello in gesso
pedestrian croswalk	strisce pedonali	plate	piatto
pen	penna	platform	binario
penalty area	area di rigore	player	giocatore
pencil	mattita	please	per favore/per piacere/per cortesia
pencil sharpener	temperamatite		
pendant	ciondolo	Please (here you are).	Prego.
penicillin	penicillina	Please hold.	Stia in linea.
performance	rappresentazione	pneumonia	polmonite
perfume	profumo	pocket	tasca
perfume store	profumeria	pocket calculator	calcolatrice
petunia	petunia	poetry	poesia
pharmacist	farmacista	police officer	polizotto
pharmacy	farmacia	police	polizia
phonebook	elenco telefonico	Polish	polacco
phone number	numero di telefono	pool	biliardi
		pool	piscina
photography	fotografia	poor	povero
piano	pianoforte	popular	popolare
piece of cake	fetta di torta	pork	maiale
piece of paper	foglio di carta	Portuguese	portoghese
pill	pastiglia	post	palo
pillow	cuscino	post office box	casella postale
pilot	pilota	postage	affrancatura
pin	spillo		

postal clerk	impiegato postale		**Really?**	Davvero?
postcard	cartolina postale		**Really?**	Sul serio?
postman	postino		**rearview mirror**	specchietto
pregnant	incinta		**receipt**	ricevuta
prescription	ricetta		**receptionist**	receptionist
president	presidente		**red**	rosso
printed matter	stampe		**referee**	arbitro
printer	stampante		**refrigerator**	frigorifero
producer	produttore		**register**	fare una raccomandata
production	messa in scena		**register letter**	raccomandata
program	programma		**remedy**	rimedio
prophylactics	preservativi		**researcher**	ricercatore
punch	perforatore		**reservation**	prenotazione
purple	viola		**restaurant**	ristorante
rabbit	coniglio		**restaurant (small)**	trattoria
race	gara		**restaurant car**	carrozza ristorante
radiator	termosifone			
radio	radio		**resume**	CV/curriculum
radish	ravanello		**reverse charges**	a carico del destinatario
railway	ferrovia			
rain	pioggia		**rib**	costola
raincoat	impermeabile		**rich**	ricco
rainstorm	temporale		**right (direction)**	destra
raise	aumento di stipendio		**ring**	anello
rake	rastrello		**ring finger**	anulare
rare	al sangue		**rock music**	musica rock
raspberry	lampone		**roof**	tetto
raspberry sherbet	sorbetto ai lamponi		**room**	camera
			room	stanza
			root	radice

root canal work	trattamento della radice
rose	rosa
rough, coarse	rozzo
round-trip ticket	biglietto andata e ritorno
rowing	canotaggio
ruby	rubino
rug	tappeto
ruler	riga
rush hour	ora di punta
Russian	russo
sad	triste
salad	insalata
salad bowl	insalatiera
salary	salario
sale	saldi
same	stesso
sandals	sandali
sapphire	zaffiro
Saturday	sabato
saucepan	pentola
sausage	salsiccia
saxophone	sassofono
scalp massage	frizione
scanner	scanner
scarf	sciarpa
scenery	scenario
school	scuola
scientist	scienzato
Scottish	scozzese
sculpture	scultura

seafood	frutti di mare
search engine	motore di ricerca
seasickness	mal di mare
seat	posto
seatbelt	cintura di sicurezza
second class	seconda classe
second course	secondo (piatto)
second floor (U.S.), first floor (Italy)	primo piano
secretary	segretaria
security check	controllo di sicurezza
See you . . .	Ci vediamo . . .
sender	mittente
separated	separato
September	settembre
service charge	servizio
set of drawers	cassettiera
shampoo	shampoo
sheets	lenzuola
shelf	scaffale
shirt	camicia
shirt (jersey)	maglia
shoelace	laccio
shoes	scarpe
short	basso
short	corto
short pass	passaggio corto
shoulder	spalla

shovel	pala	sleeping compartment	cuccetta
show	spettacolo	sleeve	manica
shower	doccia	slender	snello
shower curtain	tenda da doccia	slippers	pantofole
shower in the room	con bagno	small	piccolo
shutter	imposta	small parcel	pacchetto
shuttle	shuttle	smaller	più piccolo
sick	malato	smokers	fumatori
sideboard	credenza	smooth	morbido
silk	seta	snack	merendina
silver	argento	sneakers	scarpe da ginnastica
silver (in color), silvery	argenteo	snow	neve
silver plated	argentato	So much the better.	Tanto meglio.
silver, made of silver	d'argento	So much the worse.	Tanto peggio.
silverware	posate	soap	sapone
singer	cantante	soccer	calcio
single	celibe (m.), nubile (f.)	socks	calzini
sink	lavandino	soft	morbido
sir, Mr.	signore	soldier	soldato
sister	sorella	son	figlio
sister-in-law	cognata	song	canzone
site	sito	sore throat	faringite
size	taglia, misura	soup	zuppa, minestra, minestrone
skating	patinaggio	soup bowl	piatto fondo
skin	pelle	south	sud
skirt	gonna	Spain	Spagna
skull	cranio	Spanish	spagnolo
sleeper car	vagone letto	special delivery	espresso

special offer	offerta speciale	**stool**	sgabello
spectators	spettatori	**stop**	stop
speed limit	limite di velocità	**store**	negozio
spike heel	tacco a spillo	**storm**	tempesta
spinach	spinaci	**storm**	temporale
spine	spina dorsale	**straight ahead**	sempre diritto
spoon	cucchiaio	**strand**	frangetta
sport	sport	**strawberry**	fragola
sports	sport	**strawberry ice cream**	gelato alla fragola
sprain	strappo muscolare	**study**	studio
spring	primavera	**stupid**	stupido
stage	palcoscenico	**stupid person (Tuscany)**	bischero
stain	macchia		
staircase, stairs	scala	**stupid person, a jerk**	scemo/a
stamp (noun)	francobollo		
stamp (verb)	affrancare	**subway**	metropolitana
stamp machine	distributore francobolli	**sugar**	zucchero
		suit	completo
stapler	spillatrice	**summer**	estate
starch(ed)	inamidato	**sun**	sole
station	stazione	**Sunday**	domenica
steak	bistecca	**sunglasses**	occhiali da sole
steering wheel	volante	**supermarket**	supermercato
stepfather	patrigno	**surgeon**	chirurgo
stepmother	matrigna	**suspension file**	raccoglitore delle schede
steward/ stewardess	assistente di bordo		
		sweater	maglione
stockbroker	agente di cambio	**Swedish**	svedese
		sweeper	libero
stocking	calza	**sweets**	dolci
stomach	stomaco	**swimming**	nuoto

Swiss	svizzero
system folder	cartella sistema
table	tavola
tablecloth	tovaglia
tall	alto
tartar	tartaro
taxi	taxi
taxi stand	stazione dei taxi
team	squadra
teaspoon	cucchiaino
technician	tecnico
telegram	telegramma
telephone	telefono
telephone booth	cabina telefonica
telephone call	telefonata
telephone directory	guida telefonica
telephone number	numero di telefono
television set	televisore
teller window	cassa
temperature chart	diagramma della temperatura
temple	tempia
temporary filling	otturazione provvisoria
tennis	tennis
terminal	terminal
test	esame
Thank you.	Grazie.

Thank you very much.	Mille grazie.
That's crazy.	Roba da matti.
That's really good! (ironic)	Bell'affare!
theater	teatro
thermometer	termometro
thick	spesso
thief	al ladro
this afternoon	questo pomeriggio
this evening	stasera
throat	trachea
throw-in	rimessa laterale
thumb	pollice
Thursday	giovedì
ticket	biglietto
ticket office	biglietteria
tie	cravatta
tie score	pareggio
tight(-fitting)	stretto
tip	mancia
tire	gomma/pneumatico
tired	assonnato
title	titolo
to	a
to act	recitare
to age badly	portare male gli anni
to applaud	applaudire
to ask a question	fare una domanda

to be	essere	to be worth the trouble	valere la pena
to be afraid (of)	avere paura (di)	to be wrong, incorrect	avere torto
to be at stake	essere in gioco	to be _____ years old	avere + number + anni
to be broke	essere al verde		
to be called	chiamarsi	to become sexually excited	arrapare
to be cold	avere freddo	to bleed	sanguinare
to be cold (weather)	fare freddo	to blow dry	asciugare con il phon
to be fixated on something	avere un chiodo fisso in testa	to board	imbarcare
to be hot (weather)	fare caldo	to break one's arm, leg	rompersi il braccio/la gamba
to be hungry	avere fame		
to be in a hurry	avere fretta	to brush	spazzolare
to be made fun of	preso in giro	to brush (one's teeth)	spazzolarsi i denti
to be on one's guard	stare in guardia	to buckle one's seat belt	allacciare la cintura di sicurezza
to be out of one's mind	essere un po' di fuori		
to be out of one's mind	fuori di testa	to build, to construct	costruire
to be outside	stare fuori	to button up	abbottonare
to be right, correct	avere ragione	to buy a ticket	fare il biglietto
to be sleepy	avere sonno	to call	chiamare, telefonare a
to be standing	stare in piedi	to call back	richiamare
to be thirsty	avere sete	to cash (a check)	incassare un assegno
to be warm (hot)	avere caldo	to change	cambiarsi
to be well/ unwell	stare bene/male	to cheat	barare
to be with	stare con	to cheat or swindle somebody	fregare

to check bags	consegnare i bagagli	**to download**	scaricare
to clap	applaudire	**to draw**	disegnare
to clean	pulire	**to dress (oneself), to get dressed**	vestirsi
to clean/brush one's teeth	lavarsi i denti		
to click	cliccare	**to drink**	bere
to close	chiudere	**to drive**	guidare
to close/shut the curtains	chiudere le tende	**to drive someone crazy**	fare impazzire
to comb	pettinare	**to dry**	asciugare
to comb one's hair	pettinarsi	**to dry clean**	lavare a secco
to cook	cucinare/ cuocere	**to dump someone**	mollare qualcuno
to cough	tossire	**to dye/to color**	tingere
to cross	attraversare	**to eat**	mangiare
to curl	arricciare i capelli	**to enjoy oneself**	divertirsi
		to examine	visitare
to cut	tagliare	**to extract**	estrarre
to cut it short	per farla breve	**to faint**	svenire
to dance	ballare	**to fall**	cadere
to daydream	essere nelle nuvole	**to fall asleep**	addormentarsi
		to fall in love	innamorarsi
to dial the number	fare il numero	**to feel**	sentirsi
		to feel like	avere voglia di
to die of boredom	morire dalla noia	**to fill it up**	fare il pieno
		to fire	licenziare
to do someone's hair	fare i capelli	**to fit; to suit**	stare bene (a)
to do the washing/ laundry	fare il bucato	**to get a ticket**	prendere una multa
		to get angry	arrabbiarsi
		to get bored	annoiarsi
to do, to make	fare	**to get dressed**	vestirsi

to get gas	fare benzina	**to knot, to tie**	annodare
to get married	sposarsi	**to land**	atterrare
to get ready	prepararsi	**to leave**	partire
to get up, to rise	alzarsi	**to leave a message**	lasciare un messaggio
to give a gift	fare un regalo	**to lie down**	sdraiarsi
to give a ticket	dare una multa	**to listen (to)**	ascoltare
to go	andare	**to listen to music**	ascoltare la musica
to go food shopping	fare la spesa	**to lose**	perdere
to go for a ride	fare un giro	**to lose a tooth**	perdere un dente
to go shopping	fare le spese	**to make a mistake**	fare un errore
to go to bed	andare a letto		
to go to sleep	addormentarsi	**to make a reservation**	fare una prenotazione
to hang up	riagganciare	**to matter, to have at heart**	stare a cuore
to hang up	riattaccare		
to hang up the wash/laundry	stendere il bucato	**to measure**	misurare
		to mend	rammendare
to have	avere	**to need medicine**	avere bisogno di medicina
to have breakfast	fare colazione		
to have high blood pressure	avere l'ipertensione	**to need, have need of**	avere bisogno di
		to open	aprire
to have low blood pressure	avere l'ipotensione	**to open/draw the curtains**	aprire le tende
to hire	assumere		
to hitchhike	fare l'autostop	**to operate**	operare
to improvise	improvvisare	**to order**	ordinare
to iron	stirare	**to paint**	dipingere, verniciare
to irritate or annoy	scocciare		
		to park	parcheggiare
to keep quiet	stare zitto	**to pass (overtake)**	sorpassare
to kick	calciare		

to pay attention	fare attenzione
to pay attention	stare attento
to perm	fare la permanente
to play	giocare a
to play by ear	suonare a orecchio
to play by sight	suonare a prima vista
to play the guitar	suonare la chitarra
to play the piano	suonare il pianoforte
to prefer	preferire
to pull out	estrarre
to pull over to the side of the road	accostare
to rain	piovere
to rape	violentare
to read	leggere
to reboot	rifare il booting
to relax	riposarsi
to remove	estrarre, togliere
to rent	affittare
to repair	riparare, rammendare
to repeat	ripetere
to restart	riavviare
to ring	squillare
to ring	suonare
to rinse	sciacquare
to score a goal	fare un gol

to see	vedere
to sew	cucire
to shave	fare la barba/ radere
to show off	fare il grande
to shut up, to shut one's trap	chiudere il becco
to sign	firmare
to sing	cantare
to sit down	sedersi or accomodarsi
to sleep	dormire
to slow down	rallentare
to sneeze	starnutire
to speak	parlare
to stand (sit) up straight	stare su
to stand aside	starsene da parte
to stop (oneself)	fermarsi
to switch on	accendere
to take a bath	fare il bagno
to take a break	fare una pausa
to take a picture	fare una foto
to take a short trip	fare una gita
to take a shower	fare la doccia
to take a trip	fare un viaggio
to take a walk	fare una passeggiata
to take off	decollare
to take off	togliere

to tease	cotonare	tonsils	tonsille
to the left	alla sinistra	too much, too many	troppo
to the right	alla destra	tooth	dente
to travel	viaggiare	toothache	mal di denti
to try	provare	toothbrush	spazzola per i denti
to turn	girare	toothpaste	dentifricio
to turn on	accendere	touch line	linea laterale
to unbutton	sbottonare	toward	verso
to understand	capire	towel	asciugamano
to undo	sbottonare	toy store	negozio di giocattoli
to undress (oneself)	spogliarsi	tracks	binari
to varnish	verniciare	traffic lights	semaforo
to vomit	vomitare	tragedy	tragedia
to wage war	fare la guerra	train	treno
to wake up	svegliarsi	train station	stazione
to want	avere voglia di	tranquilizer	tranquillante
to wash	lavare	traveler's check	travelers check, assegno turistico
to wash (oneself), to wash up	lavarsi	trim	spuntatina
to win	vincere	trombone	trombone
to work	lavorare	truck	camion
to x-ray	fare una radiografia	trumpet	tromba
to yield	dare la precedenza	trunk	bagagliaio
toaster	tostapane	T-shirt	maglietta
tobacco shop	tabaccaio	Tuesday	martedì
toilet	toilette	tulip	tulipano
toilet paper	carta igienica	turkey	tacchino
tomorrow	domani	turn left	gira a sinistra
tongue	lingua	turn right	gira a destra

two beds	due letti
two nights	due notti
two people	due persone
ugly	brutto
ulcer	ulcera
umbrella	ombrello
uncle	zio
under	sotto
underwear	biancheria intima
underwear	mutande
unemployed	disoccupato
unemployment	disoccupazione
United States	Stati Uniti
university	università
unpleasant	antipatico
unstamped	non affrancato
vacuum cleaner	aspirapolvere
validate	timbrare
value declaration	dichiarazione del valore
vanilla ice cream	gelato alla vaniglia
vase	vaso
vaseline	vaselina
VCR	videoregistratore
veal	vitello
vegetable course	contorno
vegetable garden	orto
vein	vena

velvet	velluto
Very nice! (ironic)	Bella roba!
victory	vittoria
violin	violino
visa	visto
visiting hours	orario delle visite
volleyball	pallavolo
waiter	cameriere
waitress	cameriera
wake-up call	servizio sveglia
wall	parete
wall calendar	calendario da parete
wallet	portafoglio
wallpaper	carta da pareti
wardrobe	armadio
washing machine	lavatrice
wastepaper basket	cestino
watch	orologio
watch out	attenzione
water	acqua (minerale)
water jug	caraffa per acqua
water polo	pallanuoto
waterskiing	sci nautico
weather report	bollettino meteorologico
wedding ring	fede

Wednesday	mercoledì
weed	erbaccia
well done	ben cotto
west	ovest
what	che
What a mess.	Che macello.
What's your name? (formal)	Come si chiama Lei?
What's your name? (informal)	Come ti chiami?
What's the matter with you?	Che ti passa per la testa?
when	quando
where	dove
Where are you from?	Di dove sei?
Where is . . . ?/ Where are . . . ?	Dov'è . . . ?/Dove sono . . . ?
whipped cream	panna montata
white	bianco
who	chi
why	perché
widowed	vedovo
wife	moglie
wig	parrucca
window	finestra
window	finestrino
windshield	parabrezza
windshield wipers	tergicristalli
wine	vino

wine jug	brocca per vino
winter	inverno
wisdom tooth	dente del giudizio
wisp	ciocca di capelli
wisteria	glicine
with	con
with a credit card	con la carta di credito
with traveler's checks	con i travelers check
without	senza
wool	lana
worn out	consumato
wound	ferita
wrist	polso
writer	scrittore
yard	giardino
yellow	giallo
yes	sì
yogurt	yogurt
young	giovane
You don't say!	A chi lo dici!
You're welcome.	Prego. or Non c'è di che.
zinnia	zinnia
zipper	cerniera

Appendix C

Essential Words and Phrases

This quick reference section will help you with the basics. Use it if you're in too much of a hurry to flip through an entire chapter.

Meeting People

yes	*sì*
	see
no	*no*
	noh
Thank you.	*Grazie.*
	GRAHTS-ee-eh
You're welcome.	*Prego.*
	pray-goh
Please . . .	*Per favore . . .*
	pehr fah-VOH-reh
Excuse me . . .	*Mi scusi . . .*
	mee skoo-zee
Hello.	*Salve.*
	sahl-vay
Goodbye.	*Arrivederci.*
	ahr-ree-veh-DEHR-cheeh
Good morning.	*Buon giorno.*
	bwohn johr-noh
Goodnight.	*Buona notte.*
	bwoh-nah noht-teh
I do not understand.	*Non capisco.*
	nohn kah-PEES-koh
Do you speak English?	*Parla inglese?*
	pahr-lah een-GLEH-say
What is your name?	*Come si chiama?*
	koh-meh see KYAH-mah
Nice to meet you.	*Felice di conoscerLa.*
	feh-LEE-cheh dee koh-NOH-shehr-lah
How are you?	*Come sta?*
	koh-meh stah

good	*bene*
	beh-neh
bad	*male*
	mah-leh

Directions

map	*mappa*
	mahp-pah
left	*sinistra*
	see-nees-trah
right	*destra*
	des-trah
straight ahead	*diritto*
	dee-REET-toh
far	*lontano*
	lohn-TAH-noh
near	*vicino*
	vee-CHEE-noh

Transportation

Where is it?	*Dove si trova?*
	doh-veh see troh-vah
How much is the fare?	*Quanto costa il biglietto?*
	kwahn-toh kohs-tah eel beel-YEHT-toh
ticket	*biglietto*
	beel-YEHT-toh
A ticket to. . . , please.	*Un biglietto a . . . , per favore.*
	oon beel-YEHT-toh pehr-fah-voh-ray
Where do you live?	Dove abita?
	doh-veh AH-bee-tah

train	*treno*	
	tray-noh	
bus	*autobus*	
	OHW-toh-boos	
subway	*metropolitana*	
	meh-troh-poh-lee-TAH-nah	
airport	*aeroporto*	
	ah-eh-roh-POHR-toh	
train station	*stazione del treno*	
	stahts-YOH-neh dehl tray-noh	
bus station	*stazione degli autobus*	
	stahts-YOH-neh dehl-yee	
	OHW-toh-boos	
subway station	*stazione della metropolitana*	
	stahts-YOH-neh dehl-lah meh-troh-	
	poh-lee-TAH-nah	
departure	*partenza*	
	pahr-TEHN-zah	
arrival	*arrivo*	
	ahr-REE-voh	
parking	*parcheggio*	
	pahr-KEHJ-joh	

Accommodations

hotel	*hotel*	
	oh-tell	
room	*camera*	
	KAH-meh-rah	
reservation	*prenotazione*	
	preh-noh-tahts-YOH-neh	

Do you have a room available?	*Avete una camera libera?* ah-veh-teh oo-nah KAH-meh-reh LEE-beh-rah
no vacancies	*niente camere libere* nyehn-teh KAH-meh-rah LEE-beh-reh
passport	*passaporto* pah-sah-POHR-toh

Around Town

bank	*banca* bahn-kah
church	*chiesa* kyeh-zah
hospital	*ospedale* ohs-peh-DAH-lay
museum	*museo* moo-zeh-oh
pharmacy	*farmacia* fahr-mah-CHEE-ah
post office	*ufficio postale* oof-FEE-choh pohs-TAH-lay
restaurant	*ristorante* rees-toh-RAHN-teh
shop	*negozio* neh-GOHTS-ee-oh
square	*piazza* pyahts-sah
street	*strada* strah-dah

Shopping

How much does this cost?	*Quanto costa?* kwahn-toh kohs-tah
I will buy it.	*Lo compro.* loh kohm-proh
I would like to buy . . .	*Vorrei comprare . . .* vohr-ray kohm-PRAH-ray
Do you have . . . ?	*Avete . . . ?* ah-veh-teh
open	*aperto* ah-pehr-toh
closed	*chiuso* kyoo-zoh
postcard	*cartolina postale* kahr-toh-lee-nah pos-TAH-leh
stamps	*francobolli* frahn-koh-BOHL-lee
little	*poco* poh-koh
a lot, many, much	*molto* mohl-toh
all	*tutto* toot-toh

Food and Beverages

beer	*birra* bee-rah
coffee	*caffè* kahf-FEH
drink	*bevanda* beh-VAHN-dah

juice	*succo*
	sook-koh
tea	*tè*
	teh
water	*acqua*
	ahk-wah
wine	*vino*
	vee-noh
dessert	*dolce*
	dohl-cheh
fish	*pesce*
	pesh-sheh
fruit	*frutta*
	froo-tah
meat	*carne*
	kahr-neh
potato	*patata*
	pah-tah-tah
salad	*insalata*
	een-sah-LAH-tah
vegetable	*legumi*
	leh-GOO-mee

Index